ABOUT THE AUTHOR

Andrena Liu, Certified Self-Love & Life Coach and Author of *Reclaim Your Power* is a Gen Z entrepreneur and personal coach for many people on their journey to transforming their lives. She is passionate about helping individuals become empowered in themselves with confidence, self-love, healing and wellness.

Andrena was born and raised in Canada. Since 2022, she has been traveling worldwide living as a digital nomad. She offers self-love and life coaching services to those looking to improve their self-love, self-worth and personal lives. Her social media platforms are constantly refreshed with new

Andrena Liu

motivational, inspirational and educational content for those on their own self-growth journeys.

RECLAIM YOUR POWER

DEDICATION

This book is dedicated to all its readers and anyone in the same position as the one I used to be in.

I also dedicate this book to my two younger sisters, Tina and Katrina. I love you both so much, and I hope these insights and wisdoms inspire you two to create positive life-changing decisions.

This book is also dedicated to my dear brother Tom whom I treasure deeply.

I also want to dedicate this book to my entire family and all my friends. Thank you for being part of my journey.

A very special person, my soul sister Jenny – this book is also dedicated to you.

This book is also dedicated to my therapist, Anne, who has taught me so much and has been an inspiration and guiding light for me.

I also dedicate this book to my elementary school counselor, Mrs. Penz, who was there to support me through my childhood after my mom had passed away. Thank you for your kindness and empathy.

This book is also dedicated to my younger self, my inner child, the one who didn't know any better but had to learn on her own through trial and error.

May this book inspire you and all of its readers to look after yourself and advocate for yourself the way you truly deserve.

THANK YOU

This book and all the insights within it extend beyond my own inner wisdoms. I would not be the person I am today, neither would I have written this book if it weren't for the support I've received through my years of life. I extend my deepest gratitude to all my teachers, mentors, counselors and therapists who have guided me through life and walked this path before me. I also give credit and thanks to all the authors of other self-help books I've indulged in during my never-ending personal growth journey. I do not claim all the ideas in this book as my own, and I give full credit and thanks to the ones who have taught me the many life lessons and valuable techniques I'm about to share in this book.

Andrena Liu

RECLAIM
YOUR
POWER

The power of self-love: Attain inner peace, strengthen relationships & live a life of fulfilment

ANDRENA LIU

Andrena Liu

© Andrena Liu 2024 All rights reserved.

No part of this publication may be copied or reproduced in any format without prior consent from the copyright owner and author of this book.

RECLAIM YOUR POWER

Table of Contents

INTRODUCTION 11

ONE: WHAT IS SELF-LOVE & WHY IS IT EVEN IMPORTANT 19

TWO: WHY SELF–LOVE ISN'T SELFISH 27

THREE: HOW TO PRACTICE SELF-LOVE 35

FOUR: HEALING YOUR PAST & PRESENT 57

FIVE: BOUNDARIES 85

SIX: SELF-LOVE FOR GRIEF AND LOSS 95

SEVEN: SELF-LOVE IN THE ROLE OF FORGIVENESS 117

EIGHT: SELF-ACCEPTANCE FOR ALL THAT YOU ALREADY ARE 137

NINE: A HOLISTIC APPROACH TO SELF-LOVE 145

TEN: BONUS: FREE SELF-LOVE BOOSTING TOOLS 161

CONCLUSION 169

THE END OF A BOOK; THE BEGINNING OF AN EVOLUTION 169

"A coach and leader isn't someone who hasn't suffered or made mistakes themselves. They are the ones who have been down in the trenches and come out on the other side, inspired to help guide others who are in a position they once were in."
- *Andrena Liu*

INTRODUCTION

Author's Inspiration

It all began at the age of 4 when my mother passed away. I was left to grow up without a mother to teach me how to look after myself. Throughout my young years, I developed people-pleasing tendencies, did not learn to have any boundaries, was taken advantage of, and struggled with low self-worth.

The moment where everything changed for me was when I embarked on my spiritual journey and personal development path. I became committed to taking care of my entire holistic being. I grew an obsession over health, nutrition, fitness, educating myself, financial literacy, improving my habits and rituals, introspection and reflection, doing shadow work, investigating my triggers and patterns and breaking out of my unhealthy cycles.

I started documenting this journey on TikTok, where my videos went viral, and I started growing a loyal audience that was inspired by my insights. Before I knew it, people were reaching out to me in DM's seeking advice on their own situations and I held space for them. By then, I was coaching in my DM's for free without even realizing it.

Self-love was the key to breaking free from my traumas and bad habits. Self-love was the remedy to a thriving mental, emotional, physical and spiritual health.

RECLAIM YOUR POWER

I wouldn't be standing here today in good happiness and health if it weren't for the life-changing decisions I made.

I wrote this book because I felt driven to put together everything I've learned about self-love, healing and personal development into one neat and tidy place. I aspire to inspire others who are also on their own journeys. Let this not feel like you are all alone in your journey of growth and healing. There are people among you who are walking similar paths, and you are not alone.

What to Expect in Each Chapter

Introduction: A full intro into why self-love is meaningful to me as the author. It explains why I felt called to write this book, and it dives further into what you can expect to read in the upcoming chapters.

Chapter 1: In the first chapter, you'll learn what self-love really means, and why it's important for everyone to practice it. This chapter pulls back the curtains on why self-love is so significant regardless of who you are and where you're at in life.

Chapter 2: This next chapter discusses the reasons why self-love is not narcissistic or selfish, but actually selfless. You'll understand how filling up your own cup leads to the ability of channeling the best, most radiant version of you so others can be positively affected by you. This chapter reassures you that self-care is important if you want to show up as your best self for those around you. It is not selfish to take time for yourself when others depend on your ability to step your best foot forward.

Chapter 3: Chapter 3 is full of practical techniques and tactics on how you can start to practice self-love in your life every day. Suitable for everyone from all walks of life, these tips are meant to be applied in every-day life for life-changing results.

Chapter 4: Here, we'll dive into why it's crucial to heal your past and your present. It is everyone's own duty to do their own inner work, even to those who think they are exempt from it. Whether or not you've faced trauma in life, everyone has a bit of room for growth, improvement and healing. This chapter explores some of the subconscious limiting beliefs formed from past events that may be hindering your growth and success. We'll learn about triggers, how to identify them, and how to work backwards to heal from our triggers through inner child healing.

Chapter 5: In Chapter 5, we'll go over personal boundaries that can be applicable to many every-day scenarios to protect your mental, physical and emotional well-being. There will be examples of assertive communication where you can learn how to voice your boundaries without sounding confrontational.

Chapter 6: This chapter involves how the practice of self-love can be applied in the context of navigating grief and loss. These themes are inevitable in our human experience, and self-love can play a big part in promoting healing during those challenging dark times.

Chapter 7: We'll discuss how self-love can be used in forgiveness in Chapter 7. Holding onto resentment towards others and yourself can have a detrimental impact to your mental and emotional health. It can feel debilitating when you carry bitterness on your tongue from what others have done to you, or for the mistakes you've made yourself. Self-love is the way out, and forgiveness is the key.

Chapter 8: Self-love involves pursuing continuous self-improvement. But on the opposite end of that lies the delicate balance of self-acceptance for all that you already are. This is what self-love really is. It's a balance of striving to be better, yet giving yourself grace for being a perfectly flawed human being. In Chapter 8, we'll be discussing all the ways you can learn to love and accept yourself for being who and where you already are.

Chapter 9: Here, we'll be discussing the core components that make up self-love from a holistic perspective. This is a deeper dive into what self-love can look like in all arenas of life. You'll also find a hands-on journalling activity where you can craft your own plan on how you can apply self-love to your life in a holistic way. This journey looks different for everyone, so this is your chance to design a routine and personal commitments that work best for you.

Chapter 10: The final chapter is a bonus chapter holding my library of top self-love boosting tools. There, you will find my favourite curated tactics that you can immediately start applying to your life to cultivate greater self-love.

I hope you gain something inspirational and useful from this book, whether it's the desire to commit to a better you or a stronger sense of self. I went through my own personal journey of discovering self-love, and only wanted to wrap it up into a valuable gift to you.

When all is said and done, this book aims to help you to:
- Feel better about yourself and radiate confidence
- Become happier, healthier and at peace with you and your life
- Feel relief from the weight of your struggles
- Be free from other people's expectations of you
- Live life on YOUR OWN terms
- Have a good balance between family, friends, work and life
- Feel more well-rested
- Have your own cup filled
- Be in a better mental and emotional state of mind
- Be and feel calmer in any situation
- Be more productive because you are well-rested and energized

RECLAIM YOUR POWER

Are you ready to reclaim your power and cultivate your own inner source of happiness? Let's dive in.

"Wisdom isn't measured by the number of years of your life, but the trials, triumphs and lessons learned through life."
- *Andrena Liu*

CHAPTER ONE

WHAT IS SELF-LOVE & WHY IS IT EVEN IMPORTANT

What Is Self-Love & Why Is It Even Important?

Self-love is the practice of valuing and caring for yourself. It involves recognizing your worth, treating yourself with kindness, and maintaining a positive and healthy relationship with yourself. Self-love is not about being selfish or narcissistic, but about ensuring your own well-being and happiness.

Self-care is not just:
- Bubble baths
- Massages
- Spas
- Face masks
- Pampering yourself

Self-care is also:
- Investigating your triggers and healing your inner child and your internal wounds
- Drawing healthy boundaries to protect your mental and emotional wellbeing
- Staying hydrated
- Consuming a healthy balanced diet
- Eliminating bad habits
- Leaving situations and people who zap your energy
- Working on your long-term goals
- Improving your financial literacy and managing your finances responsibly

Self-love is about standing up for yourself and being your own biggest advocate.

RECLAIM YOUR POWER

Self-love is knowing you have the inherent right for good emotional, mental, physical and spiritual health, and inner peace.
Self-love is being the initiator of claiming that health and happiness that you deserve.

Self-Love Is Life-Changing

Your relationship with yourself is the most important relationship you'll ever have. You are birthed into this world by yourself, and when you die, you also die on your own. You start this life by yourself, you are the only one who is constantly with you every moment of your life and when you leave, you are the only one who is sure to be with yourself. You are the only person who lives with you 24/7, every minute of the day for your entire life. There is no one else but you.

Self-love is many things. It starts with self-awareness, knowing yourself inside and out. But expanding past that to self-acceptance, accepting all parts of yourself without judgment, but with love. Self-love is an internal acceptance for who you are, that you don't need other people's validation or approval, you have your own internal source of self-validation.

Expanding on self-awareness: Self-love is knowing your boundaries and tuning into your needs. Self-love is knowing that happiness, fulfillment and health is your birthright, that you don't need to earn it because you always already deserve it. It is choosing the things that deliver you happiness, fulfillment, health and wellness (by doing self-care).

It is knowing and accepting that it is okay to have to disappoint people sometimes because we have this birthright.

Self-love is not something that develops overnight or in an instant. It is an ongoing journey consisting of improving your mindset, working on your inner belief system, choosing better and healthier choices, and allowing yourself to be truly happy and fulfilled by authentically following your heart, that will naturally have you radiating confidence from the inside out.

Importance of Self-Love

Self-love significantly impacts many facets of your life, including mental health, self-esteem, relationships, motivation, personal growth, resilience and your overall well-being. It carries a holistic affect that can really uplevel your life.

Mental health: Practicing self-love can help in reducing stress, anxiety and depression. It promotes a positive mindset and emotional resilience.

Self-esteem: By loving yourself, you build confidence and self-worth, leading to a more positive self-image.

Healthy relationships: When you love yourself, you set healthy boundaries and are less likely to tolerate toxic relationships. It also allows you to love others more genuinely.

Motivation and growth: Self-love encourages you to pursue your goals and dreams. It motivates you to take care of your physical, emotional, and mental health.

Resilience: It helps you bounce back from setbacks and challenges, fostering a sense of inner strength and determination.

Overall well-being: Practicing self-love leads to a balanced life, where you prioritize your needs and well-being alongside those of others.

Self-love is crucial for maintaining a healthy, balanced, and fulfilling life. It impacts various aspects of your existence, from mental health to relationships and personal growth.

Chapter 1 Key Points

- Key Point 1: Self-love is not just pampering yourself; it is the practice of valuing, caring for, and maintaining a positive relationship with yourself to ensure your well-being and happiness.
- Key Point 2: Your relationship with yourself is the most important relationship you'll ever have, because everything starts and ends with you. You hold the power to every action,

behavior and decision in your life. You are the only one who is constantly with you 24/7.
- Key Point 3: Self-love is important because it impacts many facets of your life: mental health, self-esteem, relationships, motivation, personal growth, resilience and your overall well-being.

"Self-love is an internal acceptance for who you are, that you don't need other people's validation or approval, you have your own internal source of self-validation."
- Andrena Liu

Andrena Liu

CHAPTER TWO

WHY SELF-LOVE ISN'T SELFISH

Negative Impacts of Neglecting Self-Care

Whether you have a high-stress position at work, or are a busy full-time student, self-care is crucial for maintaining mental health and preserving your relationships. With our busy modern schedules, it's easy to put self-care on the backburner. Whether you feel like you don't have enough time, or you believe that self-care is selfish, neglecting your health can have detrimental impacts on your life.

Lack of self-care can lead to poor mental health, depression, anxiety, stress, fatigue, decreased motivation, physical health problems, burnout and even relationship issues. When stress builds up, our levels of patience and tolerance go down and we become more easily irritable. This can strain our personal relationships and affect our overall happiness. If family and health are even relatively important to you, then self-care should be on your to-do list.

Why Self-Love Isn't Selfish

Self-love is not selfish, vanity or narcissistic at all, so don't worry that you are being selfish, because you aren't. You have every right to stick up for yourself, and in fact, it is best for not just you but other people as well if you can be your own best advocate.

Choosing self-love can actually be self-LESS, because when you are happy, you can spread your good energy to uplift others.

RECLAIM YOUR POWER

When you have helped yourself, you can help others.

When you have healed yourself, you can now hold space for other people who may be struggling.

When you do the inner work, you change how other people experience you in their lives.

Self-love improves you so you can create a more positive impact on the world.

This is your reassurance that it's okay to do a little self-care or to take a break. Especially if there are people who depend on you, they depend on the best version of you. It is your duty to look after yourself so you can be your best version of yourself to others.

Lucy's Story

Lucy was a young remote agency worker who worked from home for a startup agency. She lived with her boyfriend who also worked from home. In this startup agency, there were heavy demands and pressures to deliver work on strict deadlines. Since she worked at a small startup, she found herself wearing multiple hats at her job, and took on more work than she had initially signed up for. Because she was young, she was determined to prove her worth. She wanted to prove that she had what it takes to be successful at her job, so she committed herself fully to work. She often worked evenings and weekends just to stay ahead.

After several months of grinding out work overtime, she was neglecting her health and became easily irritable and bitter. Since she worked from home, she often snapped at her boyfriend because she was so worn and easily agitated. She had the limiting belief that self-care was selfish. She didn't prioritize her well-being and was headed towards burnout.

Due to her easily irritable mood swings, her relationship with her boyfriend was strained. They were having relationship issues at home because she had low patience and a low threshold for tolerance. It was a breaking point for Lucy. If she continued to neglect self-care, she might sabotage her relationship entirely causing a separation and a need to relocate. This devastated Lucy because she couldn't bring herself to take time for herself even though her relationship and living situation depended on it.

RECLAIM YOUR POWER

One night while scrolling through Instagram late at night, Lucy came across a post that intrigued her. The post discussed the many ways neglecting self-care can lead to burnout and strained relationships. This sounded exactly like what Lucy was experiencing, so she read about it some more. Inspired by some of the insights and tips from this post, she started applying some boundaries at work. She became clear when she had reached her maximum bandwidth, turning down projects that she once would've said yes to. She began clocking out right at 5pm and putting her work away in the evenings and weekends. She even developed her own self-care routine that involved walking around the neighbourhood park and spending some nights in a bathtub listening to music.

Within a month, her mood became visibly better. Lucy felt her energy and joy returning. The light within her was slowly becoming restored. She realized that by caring for herself, she had more to give to those around her. Rather than snapping at her boyfriend, she became much calmer and warm in her demeanours. Her relationships improved as she became more present and engaged. Even though she was no longer taking on every project presented to her and responding to every email and message after work hours, she still managed to deliver quality work. She found that this new self-care routine had brought her greater focus and efficiency, improving her performance at work. Not only did she notice an improvement with her ability to deliver better work, but she also restored her personal relationships at the same time.

Lucy learned that self-love wasn't about being selfish; it was about replenishing her spirit so she could continue to spread kindness and love. In taking care of herself, she discovered a deeper, more sustainable happiness, enriching not only her own life but also the lives of those she cared about.

In this story, the simple mindset switch of accepting self-care as necessary changed the trajectory of her life. If she had continued to neglect her health, she would have faced a separation from her relationship, causing her to have to move apartments. By choosing self-care and looking after her health, she managed to not only save her relationship but also improve her work performance.

Chapter 2 Key Points

- **Key Point 1:** Self-love isn't selfish, vanity or narcissism. It's selfless and self-preservation.
- **Key Point 2:** Self-care is necessary for you to replenish yourself so you can show up as the best version of you to those around you who are affected by you.
- **Key Point 3:** A lack of self-care can lead to fatigue, mental health issues, decreased performance, burnout and relationship strains.

"Self-love isn't selfish. It's self-preservation. It is necessary to fill up your own cup so you can show up as the best version of you for those around you who are affected by you.
- Andrena Liu

CHAPTER THREE

HOW TO PRACTICE SELF-LOVE

1. Listen to your body and tune into your needs.

If your mind and body needs a break, allow yourself to take a break. If you're feeling overstimulated in an environment, either get away or use self-care tactics. If you're thirsty, don't just ignore your body's cue. Go drink some water. If you're feeling fatigued, you might be needing a nourishing meal. If you're sleep-deprived, make it a priority to catch up on some much-needed sleep. If you're feeling stressed or anxious, counter that with a healthy stress-management activity like walking in nature, exercising or journaling your thoughts. If you're feeling sluggish, your body may be telling you to get up and go for a jog or take a cold shower.

By tuning into your body, you develop self-awareness. With self-awareness, you now have the awareness to then communicate your needs to others. It is always good to communicate your needs, there is no harm in doing so.

Part of listening to your body ties into developing your own self-awareness over what you're comfortable with and where your limits are. This is where boundaries come into place. We'll be covering more about what boundaries are and how to apply them in Chapter 5.

2. Adopt a supportive mindset, eliminate negative self-talk and replace them with more compassionate words.

▸ *Separate yourself from your harsh inner critic.*

RECLAIM YOUR POWER

Identify your harsh inner critic whenever it appears. Your harsh inner critic may have a very clear voice that berates you and shames you. But sometimes, it's just a quiet feeling of unworthiness that doesn't make as much sound.

Learn to become aware of whenever your thoughts or feelings don't feel supportive or empowering. Then, separate yourself from it. Separate yourself from its negative claims and know that they are just independent thoughts and emotions. Those thoughts are not you.

▸ ***Be your own best friend.***

One of my favourite lines to tell my clients and other people is "be your own best friend."

In the same way that you would offer your own best friend love, compassion, understanding, support, encouragement, empowerment and advice, do the same for yourself.

Treat yourself with the same love and kindness you would offer to your own best friend.

→ *Try this...*

If you're in need of some encouragement, empowerment or love, try going in front of the mirror and telling yourself the things you need to hear as if you're a second person speaking to yourself. It may feel awkward at first if you've never tried it, but this one tool is actually incredibly powerful and effective.

▸ **"Reframing" perspectives is key.**

Reframe negative thinking and limiting beliefs to more empowering, supportive perspectives. Learn to recognize when the thoughts inside your head aren't serving you.

There are 10 common cognitive distortions that people often fall into. Cognitive distortions are irrational thought patterns that can lead to negative emotions and behaviors.

Psychiatrist, Aaron T. Beck, first introduced the concept of cognitive distortions in the 1960s. David D. Burns, psychologist and student of Beck, later popularized them, especially through his book "Feeling Good: The New Mood Therapy" in the 1980s.

As I list the definitions of the 10 common cognitive distortions, take the time to reflect on past incidences where you may have fallen into this type of thinking, and write down the cognitive distortion you had. This is great practice to help you recognize some of these negative thinking patterns so you can eventually swap them out for more supportive statements.

After each definition, you will find an example, then an example of a better alternative, followed by a line for you to write out a cognitive distortion you've encountered in the past. The last line is for you to re-write your own negative thought into a more empowering and supportive statement. This is called *reframing*.

✧ *Self-Awareness Practice* ✧

1) All-or-Nothing Thinking (Black-and-White Thinking): Viewing situations in only two categories instead of on a continuum.

Example: "If I can't do this task perfectly, I might as well not do it at all."

Empowering alternative: "Done is better than perfect. I'd rather produce some type of work than have done nothing at all."

An all-or-nothing thought I've had in the past:

_____

_____

A more empowering and supportive alternative:

_____

_____

2) Overgeneralization: Making broad interpretations from a single or few events.

Example: "I didn't get the job I interviewed for; I'll never find a good job."

Empowering alternative: "I didn't get the job I interviewed for, but that's not a reflection of my competence. There are plenty more chances out there for me."

An overgeneralization I've used in the past:

_____

_____

A more empowering and supportive alternative:

_____

_____

3) Mental Filter: Focusing on a negative detail or bad event and allowing it to taint everything else.

Example: "Despite getting compliments on my work, I can't stop thinking about that one critique I received."

Empowering alternative: "I can receive criticism as direction for my improvement, but still acknowledge all the good things that went well in my work."

A mental filter I've used in the past:

_____

_____

A more empowering and supportive alternative:

_____

_____

4) Disqualifying the Positive: Dismissing positive experiences or attributes by insisting they "don't count."

Example: "I finished the marathon, but it's not a big deal since so many people do it."

Empowering alternative: "I'm proud of myself for finishing that marathon. I know I really put a lot of commitment into it, and it wasn't easy."

A disqualification of the positive I've used in the past:

_____

_____

A more empowering and supportive alternative:

_____

_____

5) Jumping to Conclusions: Making a negative interpretation without actual evidence. It includes mind reading (assuming the thoughts and intentions of others) and fortune-telling (predicting future events).

Example: "She hasn't responded to my message in hours; she must hate me."

Empowering alternative: "She hasn't responded to my message in hours. I wonder what's happening on her end, but I won't know unless she tells me."

A jump to conclusions I've had in the past:

_____

_____

A more empowering and supportive alternative:

_____

_____

6) Magnification (Catastrophizing) or Minimization: Blowing things out of proportion or inappropriately shrinking something to make it seem less important.

Example: "I didn't make it to the gym this week; my whole fitness routine is ruined and not worth doing now."

Empowering alternative: "I didn't make it to the gym this week, but I can always start fresh tomorrow."

A magnification, catastrophizing or minimization I've used in the past:

_____

_____

A more empowering and supportive alternative:

_____

_____

7) Emotional Reasoning: Assuming that because you feel a certain way, what you think must be true.

Example: "I feel incompetent, so I must not be good enough at my job."

Empowering alternative: "I feel incompetent right now, but I know these are just feelings, and I don't choose to identify with them right now."

A time I've used emotional reasoning in the past:

_____

_____

A more empowering and supportive alternative:

_____

_____

8) Should Statements: Using "should," "ought to," or "must" statements can lead to frustration, disappointment, and feeling guilty.

Example: "My partner should always know what I need without me having to say anything."

Empowering alternative: "I'm going to choose to not expect anything so I don't get disappointed. I'll take matters into my own hands and communicate if I need anything."

A "should" statement I've used in the past:

_____

_____

A more empowering and supportive alternative:

_____

_____

9) Labeling and Mislabeling: Assigning global negative labels to oneself or others based on specific behaviors.

Example: "He completely lost his temper the other day; he's a narcissist."

Empowering alternative: "He lost his temper once, but I understand that a one-time behavior does not define someone's character entirely. I can't label or judge so soon."

A label or mislabel I've used in the past:

_____

_____

A more empowering and supportive alternative:

_____

_____

RECLAIM YOUR POWER

10) Personalization: Taking responsibility for events outside of your control, often leading to guilt, shame, and feelings of inadequacy.

E*xample: "The dinner party was a disaster; it's all my fault because I'm a bad host."*

Empowering example: "The dinner party didn't go according to plan, but there were several external factors that contributed to it and they were beyond my own control."

An example of personalization I've used in the past:

_____

_____

A more empowering and supportive alternative:

_____

_____

Great work on reflecting on some of your past cognitive distortions!

Now that you've had a bit of practice, I want you to continue to notice whenever you fall into any of these thinking patterns. Then, rather than believing the thought to be true, try reframing it in a way that is more empowering and supportive.

3. Make the right decisions.

When you're faced with moments where you have choices, choose the option that will provide you a healthier outcome, especially in the long run. You know it's best for you to eat healthier, exercise, drink more water and eliminate bad habits. Simple things like these are acts of self-love already.

Making good decisions for yourself also includes removing yourself from toxic relationships, friendships or jobs, because you know you deserve better. Remember, you are your own fighter. So stand up for yourself and fight for your own rights, because you deserve to live a happy and fulfilled life.

It's also everyone's own responsibility to be accountable for their own finances. Self-love includes learning more financial literacy if you don't already have a good grasp on it, and holding yourself accountable to managing your finances wisely.

Sometimes it's easier said than done though. You KNOW these are better decisions for yourself, but somehow you still can't bring yourself to do them. Why is that?

Change can be hard... because it takes us out of our comfort zone. It means having to change our lives, and our lifestyle. And right now, we're comfortable being where we are. We'd rather stay comfortable then change what we're doing, even if we know it's better for us.

So what's the solution? How can we bring about change for our highest good?

▸ *Reflect on the following introspective questions.*

i. What about my current state or situation feels safe and comfortable, that I'll have to let go of, if I want to upgrade to the next level?

ii. Why is my goal, my next upgrade, or the change I need to see for myself **important** *to me?*

iii. How can I make the importance of my goal bigger than my current comfort zone?

▸ *Practice getting comfortable with discomfort, every day.*

Growth requires us to endure discomfort. The practice of being comfortable with discomfort is a state of being that will take you to great lengths in your growth journey. If you want to push yourself to make the right decisions for your life, it'll require you to step out of your comfort zone and stay there.

You can practice living in discomfort by committing to do something healthy for yourself that is not easy for you to do. For example, try challenging yourself to take an ice-cold shower every day for 30 consecutive days. Those few minutes of extreme discomfort will be tremendously beneficial for your health, and it'll take you out of your comfort zone to train you to be able to tolerate that.

Being comfortable with discomfort is like a muscle that requires consistent training.

Another way to practice discomfort is to face your fears.

I teach this in my live in-person and virtual workshops all over the world, and it's based on the idea of *"feel the fear and do it anyway"*. The truth is, growth is not going to be easy or comfortable. It's completely normal to feel fear. But to be successful, you must not let that fear stop you. The activity I like to guide my clients through is this simple exercise...

✧ *"Feel The Fear & Do It Anyway" Activity* ✧

STEP 1: Close your eyes, take a deep breath, and then take 5 minutes to envision the ideal future of your life.

STEP 2: Think of 1 thing that scares you the most about it, or what you may have to commit to (or lose) in order to obtain this dream.

STEP 3: Make one promise/commitment to yourself to take ONE step to do something to "feel the fear and do it anyway". This one commitment will require you to feel the fear, but you must do it anyway, to take you one step closer to your goal.

For example, if your dream is to have your own TED talk one day, but your biggest fear currently is public speaking, then your first step may be to enroll in a public speaking practice group. Or you may host your own smaller workshops and presentations to smaller audiences. This would require you to step out of your comfort zone. It is an action and commitment that will require you to feel that fear and do it anyway.

4. Learn to enjoy your own company.

Practicing self-love means developing a relationship with yourself. As foreign as that might sound to you, the purpose is to treat yourself with the same love and care you would give to others. To nurture the relationship you have with yourself, you must learn to be comfortable and happy on your own.

Try any of these self-love activities solo, to get comfortable with enjoying your time alone:

- Dining at a restaurant
- Taking a solo trip
- Going to see a movie
- Exploring a city
- Having a picnic
- Going to a festival

Andrena Liu

It might feel weird and awkward at first, but the more you do it and practice appreciating the moment, the more you begin to learn more about yourself, trust yourself, and feel comfortable on your own. And the more you spend more time alone, the more you'll trust yourself faster with making the right decisions.

Chapter 3 Key Points

- **Key Point 1:** Listen to your body and tune into your needs. Take breaks, rest, nourish and exercise accordingly.
- **Key Point 2:** Eliminate negative self-talk with more empowering language. Separate yourself from your harsh inner critic and learn to become your own best friend.
- **Key Point 3:** Catch yourself in the 10 common cognitive distortions and reframe your thoughts to more empowering alternatives.
- **Key Point 4:** Make the right life decisions with the intention of bettering your long-term future, even if enduring it may feel uncomfortable.
- **Key Point 5:** "Work out" your discomfort tolerance muscle by putting yourself in healthy growth-supportive positions that force you to face your fears.
- **Key Point 6:** Learn to enjoy your own company by doing activities on your own.

"Be your own best friend. Offer yourself the same love, empathy, understanding and kindness you would give to a good friend."
- *Andrena Liu*

CHAPTER FOUR

HEALING YOUR PAST & PRESENT

Healing Your Past & Present

Whether you come from an upbringing of trauma or a pretty typical childhood, most of us actually carry some level of trauma with us that needs to be healed.

A lot of the time, when you have subconscious beliefs that are holding you back, relationship issues, or virtually any problem in life, they can often be traced back to an earlier point in your life, where a limiting belief was instilled within you from a particular event.

For example, if you struggle with productivity, progressing in your career and reaching your goals, can you think of what beliefs might be holding you back? Is it that you might think you're incapable of being so successful? Could it be that you don't think you're smart enough or qualified? What feelings come up when you think deeply about your internal beliefs? Once you have an idea of what beliefs are holding you back, and what feelings are there for you, now trace them back to your earlier beginnings, perhaps in childhood when a parent or caregiver made you feel that way. Could it be that your parent or caregiver told you that you weren't good enough or that you were stupid?

Another example could be if you struggle when your romantic partner does or says something that is triggering to you. How are they making you feel? Can you trace back to a time in your childhood where a parent or caregiver also made you feel this way?

RECLAIM YOUR POWER

When you connect the dots between your current issues, how they make you feel, and who made you feel that way in your childhood, you begin to uncover the sources behind your early traumas that have come to hinder you today.

This is all really deep work and will require real hard work on your part, with the guidance of a licensed therapist. I highly recommend absolutely everyone to see a therapist to work on their internal wounds. Your life could radically transform when you heal the wounds you may not even know exist.

Identifying Your Subconscious Limiting Beliefs

We all carry our own subconscious limiting beliefs that are secretly holding us back in life, because we are all imperfect beings placed on this planet to learn and grow. Identifying these subconscious blocks can be difficult if you don't know where to start. But luckily, I've prepared a list of the top 50 most common limiting beliefs human beings can carry. Take a few minutes to read each one, tuning into your inner self to feel if it rings true to you. For every belief that feels true, check the box beside it. For every box you check, re-write a new empowering alternative belief on the line provided.

✧ *Top 50 Limiting Beliefs* ✧

1. ☐ I am not good enough.

   _____

   _____.

2. ☐ I don't deserve success.

   _____

   _____.

3. ☐ I am not worthy of love.

   _____

   _____.

4. ☐ I am not smart enough.

   _____

   _____.

5. ☐ I am a failure.

   _____

   _____.

RECLAIM YOUR POWER

6. ☐ I don't have enough time.

   _____

   _____.

7. ☐ I am too old/too young.

   _____

   _____.

8. ☐ Money is the root of all evil.

   _____

   _____.

9. ☐ I can't trust people.

   _____

   _____.

10. ☐ Success requires sacrificing happiness.

    _____

    _____.

11. ☐ I am not creative.

   _____

   _____.

12. ☐ I am not capable of change.

   _____

   _____.

13. ☐ I always make mistakes.

   _____

   _____.

14. ☐ People will judge me if I am successful.

   _____

   _____.

15. ☐ I don't have enough resources.

   _____

   _____.

16. ☐ I am destined to be unhappy.

_____

_____.

17. ☐ I am responsible for other people's happiness.

_____

_____.

18. ☐ I am not attractive enough.

_____

_____.

19. ☐ I need to be perfect to be loved.

_____

_____.

20. ☐ It's too late to pursue my dreams.

_____

_____.

21. ☐ I am not talented enough.

_____

_____.

22. ☐ People will leave me if I am honest about my feelings.

_____

_____.

23. ☐ I don't belong anywhere.

_____

_____.

24. ☐ I will never be able to change my habits.

_____

_____.

25. ☐ I can't handle success.

_____

_____.

RECLAIM YOUR POWER

26. ☐ I am too broken to be fixed.

   _____

   _____.

27. ☐ I need to fit in to be accepted.

   _____

   _____.

28. ☐ I am not capable of making a difference.

   _____

   _____.

29. ☐ I am not allowed to express my emotions.

   _____

   _____.

30. ☐ I am not strong enough to face challenges.

   _____

   _____.

31. ☐ I must keep others happy, even at my own expense.

   _____

   _____.

32. ☐ I will never be financially secure.

   _____

   _____.

33. ☐ I am not brave enough to take risks.

   _____

   _____.

34. ☐ I don't have the right connections to succeed.

   _____

   _____.

35. ☐ My past mistakes define me.

   _____

   _____.

36. ☐ I am not disciplined enough.

_____

_____.

37. ☐ I am not interesting enough.

_____

_____.

38. ☐ I am destined to repeat the same patterns.

_____

_____.

39. ☐ I must do everything perfectly or not at all.

_____

_____.

40. ☐ I don't have control over my life.

_____

_____.

41. ☐ I am too damaged to be loved.

_____

_____.

42. ☐ I can't prioritize myself.

_____

_____.

43. ☐ I am not worthy of forgiveness.

_____

_____.

44. ☐ I will never be happy.

_____

_____.

45. ☐ I can't ask for help.

_____

_____.

RECLAIM YOUR POWER

46. ☐ I am not responsible enough to achieve my goals.

   _____

   _____.

47. ☐ I am not destined for greatness.

   _____

   _____.

48. ☐ I must always put others before myself.

   _____

   _____.

49. ☐ I am not capable of handling success.

   _____

   _____.

50. ☐ I don't have the right to take up space.

   _____

   _____.

51. Other:

_____

_____.

52. Other:

_____

_____.

53. Other:

_____

_____.

54. Other:

_____

_____.

55. Other:

_____

_____.

RECLAIM YOUR POWER

Tactical Methods to Re-Write Your Limiting Beliefs

Now that you have an idea of your limiting beliefs and alternatives brainstormed for each one, the next step is to take consistent and intentional practice of re-wiring them in your psyche. There's a plethora of ways you can introduce these empowering alternatives to your subconscious brain. The key is *intention, consistency and repetition.* Below are 2 ways you can affirm these positive messages into your brain. Choose any of the methods below and try it daily for 33 consecutive days.

Committing to a daily practice for 33 days is important because it helps form new habits, rewires the brain by strengthening positive neural pathways, and builds momentum, making the belief or behavior more automatic and ingrained. This consistent repetition over 33 days aids in reprogramming the subconscious mind, replacing old, limiting beliefs with empowering ones, leading to lasting personal change.

Method A: Record an audio.

Instructions: Record yourself speaking your affirmations out loud using your phone. Listen to your audio once before sleeping and once upon waking. To remember to listen to your audio twice daily, you can tie it into a daily habit you already do twice a day, such as when you brush your teeth. So every time you brush your teeth in the morning and at night, you can remember to listen to your audio. Do this daily for 33 days.

Method B: 3-6-9 journaling method.

The 3-6-9 journaling method is a popular method of manifestation. The numbers 3, 6, and 9 hold special significance in manifestation and belief re-wiring, inspired by Nikola Tesla's view of them as keys to the universe. In this context, 3 represents creativity and the initiation of intentions, 6 symbolizes balance and the grounding of desires, and 9 signifies completion and spiritual enlightenment. The 3-6-9 method, which involves repeating affirmations three times in the morning, six times in the afternoon, and nine times at night, is believed to reinforce these symbolic meanings, helping to rewire the subconscious mind and manifest desired outcomes.

Instructions: Write your affirmations 3 times in the morning, 6 times in the afternoon and 9 times in the evening in a journal. Do this daily for 33 days.

RECLAIM YOUR POWER

Understanding Triggers

Triggers are events, activities, sights, sounds, scents, situations or physical sensations that elicit strong emotional responses, often connecting to past traumas. Everyone has experienced a trigger and have seen someone become triggered at some point in their life. When someone is triggered, it causes them to react in an emotional way, usually out of proportion to the actual severity of the event. When people overreact, become emotional, or react irrationally, chances are that they have been triggered.

To deepen your understanding of what triggers are, here are example scenarios of each type of trigger:

Event Trigger

Scenario: Emma is at a family gathering celebrating her cousin's wedding.
Trigger: The sight of her cousin walking down the aisle.
Reaction: Emma suddenly feels an overwhelming sense of sadness and anxiety, as the wedding reminds her of her own failed marriage and the emotional trauma associated with it.

Activity Trigger

Scenario: Mark, a successful professional, experiences sudden anxiety during a work presentation.
Trigger: While presenting, Mark is reminded of a childhood incident where he was harshly criticized by

a teacher for speaking in class.
Reaction: This triggers feelings of self-doubt, causing Mark to stumble over his words and feel insecure for a moment.

Sight Trigger

Scenario: Janet is walking through a park.
Trigger: Seeing a man who resembles her past abuser.
Reaction: She feels her heart race and her palms sweat, and she quickly leaves the park to escape the anxiety and fear.

Sound Trigger

Scenario: Lily is in a café.
Trigger: A particular song starts playing on the radio.
Reaction: Lily is flooded with sadness, as that song reminds her of the loss of a significant relationship in her life.

Scent Trigger

Scenario: Mary is browsing through a department store.
Trigger: She smells a particular perfume that a loved one who had passed used to wear.
Reaction: Tears well up in her eyes as memories of her beloved family member surfaces. She quickly loses the motivation to continue running errands as she is overcome with grief.

RECLAIM YOUR POWER

Situational Trigger

Scenario: Jessica is in a meeting where her boss is giving critical feedback.
Trigger: The tone and manner of her boss's critique.
Reaction: She feels small and worthless, mirroring the emotional abuse she received from a critical parent, leading to feelings of deep shame and anxiety.

Physical Sensation Trigger

Scenario: Suzy is in a crowded elevator.
Trigger: The sensation of being tightly packed and unable to move freely.
Reaction: Suzy feels claustrophobic and starts to hyperventilate, recalling a traumatic incident where she was trapped in a small space and couldn't escape.

Becoming Self-Aware of Your Own Triggers & Investigating Them

The first step to healing your past is to become aware of your triggers. Chances are that you experience triggers at the very least on a weekly basis, but you overlook them because they've become a normal part of your life.

Your partner nags at you again with another critique and that causes you to jump to defensiveness. A friend left your message on "read" for the past week and now you're assuming they're ignoring you even though they're just busy. A song comes on that you used to listen to with someone who was once a significant part of your life and now your mood has been dampened. You're driving past a house you used to spend a portion of your life in and that brings back bittersweet memories. You get into conflict with a team member at work and you resort to shutting down because the frustration is so intense for you.

Start to become aware of your own daily triggers by making note of them in your notes as they arise in your day-to-day life. As you go about your day, pull out your phone and type in the triggers you experience so you can train yourself to become more aware of them.

You might want to list out the scenario of what was happening at the time of the trigger, who played a part in each role of this situation, the emotions it made you feel, the memories it brought back, the thoughts that were going on in your mind, and the actions or behaviors you reacted with.

You can use this template below to list out your triggers throughout the day:

Trigger Scenario:
_____(Describe the context of the situation)_____
What triggered me:
_____

Who did what:
_____

How it made me feel:
_____

My thoughts at the time:
_____

Limiting beliefs that came up:
_____

A time in my childhood or past that made me feel the same way:
_____

Once you start to dive into investigating your triggers, you'll eventually come to realize the past events that you're still hurting from. The way you feel the negative emotions and think the limiting thoughts in your mind are connected to a past event that mirrored the same pain. The reason why you feel this so strongly and overreact is because that past event has not fully healed within you yet. It's just adding to your current pain. When past events and traumas are left to fester on their own, they don't just go away by themselves. They stack up inside you silently. They pile up onto your triggers, which is why your triggers cause such a deep emotional reaction within you. It's not the situation itself that is causing you to feel this way. It's the buildup of events that mirror this current one that is the source of all your pain.

Inner Child Healing: Healing Pain Through Your Triggers

Now that you understand what triggers are and can identify your own triggers, what's next? How do we heal from this? This is where inner child healing comes in.

Contrary to popular belief, inner child healing is not just taking up the fun activities and play time we used to love as a child. Inner child healing is much deeper than that.

The concept of an inner child is that every adult in this entire world still has an inner child within them. This inner child is a wounded child version of them that experienced pain in their past. Whenever adults become triggered, their "inner child" resurfaces. This is the reason why adults can act immature even when they're fully grown. Their inner child is wounded and has resurfaced.

Inner child wounds can hold feelings of abandonment, rejection and worthlessness that all stem from childhood experiences.

RECLAIM YOUR POWER

Inner child healing can be a complex therapeutic process. It involves acknowledging and nurturing the childlike aspect of oneself that holds unresolved emotions, memories and experiences from childhood.

I'm going to share a powerful inner child healing visualization exercise you can do whenever a trigger comes up. Use this whenever you are feeling emotionally charged from a trigger to help release the past pain that you're subconsciously holding onto. This practice helps you process your past pain and release it so you can break free emotionally. After practicing this exercise, you may still experience triggers leading back to the past painful event, but don't be disheartened. It can take several sessions of inner child healing to process and let go of traumas. Remember, this pain has been building up inside you silently throughout your whole life. So for just as long as it's been sitting inside you without you knowing, it's also going to take some time for it to get fully released as well.

Inner Child Healing Visualization

It is most effective to do this exercise when the memories and emotions are fresh in your mind and your emotions are charged up. Do this while you are feeling triggered for maximum benefit. If at any point you feel emotionless or numb, try your very best to tune back into the pain you felt at the time as a child.

Step 1: If it helps with your visualization, feel free to close your eyes. If not, you can leave them open while tuning into your imagination. Think about what triggered you and how it made you feel. What thoughts come up? Feel the emotions that surface.

Step 2: Think back to a time in your childhood where similar feelings or a similar event took place. What does this trigger remind you of? Who was involved in that childhood scenario? Was it your parents or caregivers? What happened there?

Step 3: How old were you when this happened? Give a rough estimate. Now picture that wounded child that you once were in your mind at that age, at that place and time. Paint a visual of the scene. Where were you? Were you in the kitchen, the bedroom, the living room? Continue holding onto those intense emotions, feel into them deeper. Remember the pain you felt in that moment when you were standing there as a child. Remember how intensely hurt you felt.

Step 4: Now imagine you are walking up to approach your child self as your current day adult self. Imagine crouching down to their level, looking into their eyes, holding onto their hand. Tell your wounded child self all the words you needed to hear in that moment, but never got to have. Give them the empathy, the love and the understanding your child-self needed but never got. Spend some time here and give them as much love, compassion and emotional support as he or she needed.

Step 5: Close off this practice by saying whatever last loving words your wounded child self needs to hear, then slowly open your eyes. See how you feel. Hopefully it feels as if some weight has been taken off from you.

This exercise is a process and it's going to feel painful. You'll face the negative emotions that bring severe discomfort. But feeling the emotions is necessary to move this energy through and out of you. The more intense your emotions are, the more you'll be able to release them.

Chapter 4 Key Points

- **Key Point 1:** Your subconscious limiting beliefs originate from past experiences or childhood traumas that require a level of healing.
- **Key Point 2:** Professional therapy is a strong proven method to healing past experiences so you can break free of the tendencies, habits, patterns and limiting thoughts that hold you back in life.
- **Key Point 3:** Triggers are events, activities, sights, sounds, scents, situations or physical sensations that elicit strong emotional responses, often connecting to past traumas.
- **Key Point 4:** Every adult has a wounded inner child within them. When an adult is triggered, their wounded inner child tends to surface, causing emotional and sometimes disproportionate reactions.
- **Key Point 5:** Inner child healing is a therapeutic modality used to heal traumas and past pains to ease the intensity of future triggers.

"When past events and traumas are left to fester on their own, they don't just go away by themselves. They stack up inside you silently. They pile up onto your triggers, which is why your triggers cause such a deep emotional reaction within you.

It's not the situation itself that is causing you to feel this way. It's the buildup of events that mirror this current one that is the source of all your pain."
  -   Andrena Liu

Andrena Liu

CHAPTER FIVE

BOUNDARIES

Boundaries

Boundaries are the differentiator between what you will and will not tolerate, for the sake of protecting your mental, emotional, physical and/or spiritual well-being. Boundaries differ from person to person, so no one person will have the same boundaries. Your boundaries are meant to protect your energy and time. To know your own boundaries, you must become aware of your own personal limits.

Physical Boundaries

Physical boundaries can involve how much rest you're going to give yourself, what you eat and drink, who you're okay with touching you (family, friends), and how you physically interact with others (handshake, kiss, hug, etc.).

Personal boundary scenario example:
Sarah loves her personal space and feels uncomfortable when her coworker, John, stands too close to her during conversations.

Example of assertive boundary communication:
"John, I value our conversations, but I feel more comfortable when we maintain a bit more personal space. Could we stand a little further apart when we talk?"

RECLAIM YOUR POWER

Emotional Boundaries

Emotional boundaries can be how much you're willing to share about your personal life with others, or how much you're willing to lend a listening ear to a sad friend.

Emotional boundary scenario example:
David has a friend, Mike, who often shares very personal and emotionally heavy stories with him. David finds it overwhelming and needs to set a boundary.

Example of assertive boundary communication:
"Mike, I care about you and want to support you, but I find it hard to handle very emotional stories sometimes. Can we talk about lighter topics for a while?"

Time Boundaries

Time boundaries are the limits of how long you're okay with being somewhere or doing something, whether that's spending some time out with friends, or working hard on a project.

Time boundary scenario example:
Emma is working on a tight deadline for a project. Her friend, Lisa, wants to hang out and catch up, but Emma needs to focus on her work.

Example of assertive boundary communication:
"Lisa, I'd love to catch up with you, but I'm currently

swamped with a project that needs to be finished by tomorrow. Can we reschedule our meet-up for the weekend?"

Sexual Boundaries

Sexual boundaries are how much you're comfortable with being intimate with someone, or even at all. You might be off-limits on certain interactions, or you might have boundaries regarding how far you take sexual safety.

Sexual boundary scenario example:
Alex is in a new relationship with Jordan. Jordan wants to move faster physically than Alex is comfortable with.

Example of assertive boundary communication:
"Jordan, I really like where our relationship is going, but I need to take things slower physically. Let's focus on getting to know each other better first."

Intellectual Boundaries

Intellectual boundaries relate to your thoughts, ideas, how you communicate with others and whether talking about a subject is the right time or not.

Intellectual boundary scenario example:
Rebecca is at a family gathering where her cousin, Tom, starts discussing a controversial topic she doesn't want to engage in.

RECLAIM YOUR POWER

Example of assertive boundary communication:
"Tom, I understand this topic is important to you, but I'd prefer not to discuss it right now. Let's talk about something else."

Material Boundaries

Material boundaries relate to material possessions, such as what you're willing to share with others, what you can afford to share, who you will share with, and what you're not willing to share.

Material boundary scenario example:
Lily has a friend, Sophie, who frequently asks to borrow her clothes for various events. Lily has noticed that some of her favorite pieces have come back damaged or not returned at all.

Example of assertive boundary communication:
"Sophie, I love helping you out as a friend, but I've had some issues with clothes being damaged or not returned. I've decided to keep my wardrobe for personal use only. I'm happy to help you find similar items at the store if you'd like!"

Developing Your Own Boundaries

Becoming aware of your own boundaries and limits are part of the journey of developing self-awareness and furthering self-discovery. In daily life, think about what you're okay with and what you are not. To love yourself better, be sure to voice your limits to others and stand your ground. It's your responsibility only, and no one else's, to do this for you.

The fun part about self-discovery is learning more about yourself, what you're comfortable with, and what you're not willing to tolerate. As this is different for everyone, you are the writer of your own story. You create your own rules and your own boundaries.

When To Assert Boundaries VS. When To Just Be Nice

Asserting boundaries doesn't mean that you're going to become selfish and unkind as a person. Boundaries are there just to preserve your well-being. There are certainly times where you can still be nice, kind, generous and helpful to others.

The key to knowing when to act nice versus when to draw the line is to ask yourself this:

- *Is my own cup full?*
- *Am I doing this out of genuine generosity?*
- *Do I expect something in return?*
- *Will I be happy if I receive nothing in return for doing this?*

If you are in good condition to be kind and generous to others and you expect nothing in return, then it is a positive sign that you can just give or help others freely.

If there is a chance that you expect something in return or the act of kindness is not genuine, then you might want to re-evaluate your intention behind your offer. If you're not okay with the sacrifices you'll be making, you may want to reconsider proceeding.

Sometimes not all answers are black or white. In some cases, you might agree to sacrifice or give up a part of your time, energy or resources for someone you care about. It is up to your own discernment whether this is something important to you. No one can decide for you how far you're willing to go for someone. If you decide that this person or relationship is really worth sacrificing for, you may be willing to overstep your boundaries just a bit. But if you believe that it's not worth it, then kindly assert your boundary. Weigh out each possible scenario and the pro's and con's that can come out of them. Some relationships may be worth stretching the extra mile. Asserting boundaries is most essential for those who tend to say "yes" to everyone and never form any boundaries of their own, leading to resentment or burnout.

Toxic Boundaries

At this point, we've mostly discussed how boundaries can play a positive role in protecting our well-being. However, with every tool comes a good way of using it and a bad way of enforcing it. Boundaries are a tool used for self-preservation; however, depending on our intention with it, it may not always be used for good.

Toxic boundaries are when boundaries are enforced to avoid self-accountability, handling conflict, communication, problem-solving and growth. On the surface, one may presume that they're solely trying to protect their well-being. But if used in the wrong way, it can also prevent them from facing accountability or constructive conversations.

It's important to be intentional with how you use boundaries, and not let them become an excuse to avoid conflict, accountability and communication. To ensure this, you have every right to take a break to regulate your emotions and find your grounding. But be sure to return back to the scene to sort out conflict and communicate.

Don't let boundaries become an excuse to not work on relationship-building and personal growth. Boundaries can be a helpful tool if used correctly, but be mindful of its impact the longer you use them.

Chapter 5 Key Points

- **Key Point 1:** Boundaries are personal limits set to protect one's mental, emotional, physical, and spiritual well-being, ensuring healthy and respectful interactions with others.
- **Key Point 2:** Discovering that you can have boundaries doesn't mean you need to stop being kind entirely. Determine for yourself whether your kindness is genuine with no expectations in return. If your offer is coming from pure generosity, your cup is full, you expect nothing, or the investment is worth your energy, go for it.
- **Key Point 3:** Toxic boundaries are boundaries used to avoid self-accountability, handling conflict, communication, problem-solving and personal growth.

"Don't let boundaries become an excuse to not work on relationship-building and personal growth."
-   Andrena Liu

CHAPTER SIX

SELF-LOVE FOR GRIEF AND LOSS

Andrena Liu

Self-Love as a Healthy Support for Grief & Loss

At one point or another, we all experience grief and loss at a certain point in our lives. Whether it's moving abroad and saying goodbye to your family, friends and old life, or the end of a meaningful relationship, or a sudden injury or health condition that forces us to lose our previous lifestyle. Grief and loss can show up in many forms, from many different conditions. Dealing with the difficult emotions and tragedies that come with grief isn't easy. No one gives us a life manual on how to navigate these challenging times.

Grief and loss are prominent themes in my personal life. Ever since I was a young child, I was introduced to the painful heartbreak of what it was like to lose my mother at the age of 4. My entire childhood was a period of navigating through grief. And due to the loss of a parent at a young age, psychologically I developed abandonment wounds as I entered my adult years.

Although my mother had no intention of abandoning me because it was the cancer that took her life, it still affected my psyche. I grew attachments to people and feared that one day, my loved ones will always leave. This anxious attachment and fear of abandonment made me prone to codependency.

Codependency is when you put so much of your time, energy and love into someone else, that you forget to nurture yourself and begin to lose your own identity. This tends to happen more in romantic relationships. Codependency is fueled by the fear of abandonment.

There were a few phases in my life that taught me that self-love is the key to overcoming grief and loss. One of them was realizing my codependent nature, and consciously trying to break free from it. And the other was when I entered a relationship with a partner who was avoidant, which triggered my anxious attachment, but ultimately taught me to redirect my energy and focus back onto myself rather than someone else.

Whether you also experience fear of abandonment, anxious-attachment in relationships, or are simply going through grief and loss, self-love can help ease the pain and support you through these times. As we navigate through life, it's always helpful to collect better ways of coping in our toolboxes of mental support. Allow self-love to be a healthy way to handle grief and loss in life.

What grief, loss, codependency, abandonment wounds and an anxious-attachment all have in common is losing a part of yourself. Your energy is now focused on someone or something else, and you may forget to nurture your own heart and soul.

While it's important to take the time to grieve and reflect on the meaningfulness of your loss, it's equally important to tend to your own needs at this time.

Self-Compassion & Emotional Validation

Self-love for grief and loss looks like offering yourself self-compassion.

Treat yourself with the same loving kindness and understanding that you would offer to a friend.

Validate your emotions by making space to feel them and accept them. It's okay to feel sadness, anger, confusion or any other uncomfortable emotion. Accepting the whole range of human emotions is essential in the healing process.

Emotions are energy in motion. When you suppress them and ignore them, you are not dealing with it. You are burying it deep inside you *thinking* you are dealing with it. But if you don't allow yourself to feel the emotions, you won't release them properly. One day, they will resurface from an event or situation that triggers you. To release emotions, you must feel them to go through them.

I always say, nothing is ever black or white. And I say this now, because as much as it's important to feel your emotions, it's equally important to not dwell in them for too long. Too much of anything is never a good thing. Make space to feel and release your emotions, but don't stay down in that pit for too long. Know when to draw the line and continue to move forwards and upwards in life.

The Importance of Positive Self-Dialogue

Self-love involves challenging negative self-talk and reframing it into positive, encouraging thoughts. This can help mitigate feelings of guilt or self-blame that often accompany grief.

We are all our own worst critics. But to feed ourselves unsupportive thoughts only wreaks havoc on your mental and emotional health. Sure, it's a completely positive thing to hold yourself accountable and acknowledge where you could've done better. But it's important that you don't beat yourself up over it. Learn the difference between taking accountability and bullying yourself for not doing better. There's a fine line between the two, where one can support your growth and the other can easily deteriorate it.

As you go about your day, notice how you speak about yourself, whether it's out loud in conversations or just through your inner thoughts. Do you belittle yourself for your shortcomings, even if it's "just a joke"? Your subconscious mind doesn't know the difference between what is real and what is simply a joke. Be careful of the words you use to speak about yourself and try to only use words that are supportive and encouraging.

Take Time for Self-Care

This one might seem like common sense for some people. But self-care can still be easily overlooked for people who seem to have never-ending lists of responsibilities, whether it's work or family concerns.

No matter how busy you may be or how many people rely on you, it's important to take time for self-care. Like we discussed earlier in Chapter 2, self-care is crucial to prevent burnout. It's self-preservation. To help others, you must help yourself first so you can be fully capable of supporting others.

Take the time to nurture your heart, soul, body, mind and spirit. The tactics required will look different from person to person. Maybe you need a moment to journal out your thoughts. Maybe you need to take a retreat out in nature and be in silence for a while. Maybe you need to get into an exercise practice to get the good endorphins flowing. Maybe you just need to vent to a trusted friend. Whatever it may be, truly take the time to give yourself what you need during this sensitive time.

Why Loss is so Painful

The reason why grief and loss are so painful is because when you lose something or someone, you lose a part of yourself and a part of your life with it. Parting from what you love and are familiar with isn't easy.

For most people, our lives are comprised of the following main components: Health, relationships (family, friends, S/O), hobbies/interests/leisure, personal goals, career and education. This chart might look different to others. Some might have religion included. But for the sake of general relatability, I've only included the common main parts that most people can relate to.

In a happy, thriving life, you would have all areas of this pie chart filled. Your health is in good condition. Your relationships are doing well. You have time for leisure and hobbies. You are working towards your personal goals. Your career is in motion. And you are working away at furthering your education.

The Pie Chart of Life

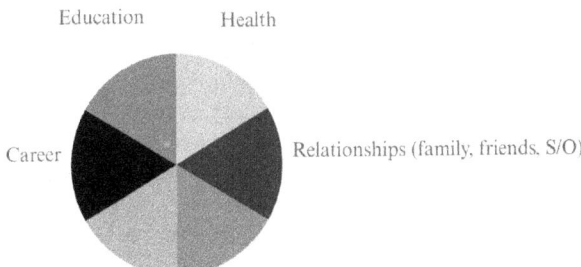

Now, the reason why the loss of a relationship is so painful is because suddenly you lose pieces of yourself and what was once your life. Maybe this significant loss put a halt to you spending time enjoying your favourite activities. Maybe it's taken a dent to your health. Maybe you've stalled in your career a bit because you can't focus on work properly.

The loss of a significant relationship creates a domino effect that leaks out into other areas on your life. In extreme cases, this may happen. But maybe it doesn't affect other parts of your life to this extent. Either way, a chunk of that pie is gone. And that's why you feel like you're left with an empty hole.

The Pie Chart of Life (With Loss of Relationship)

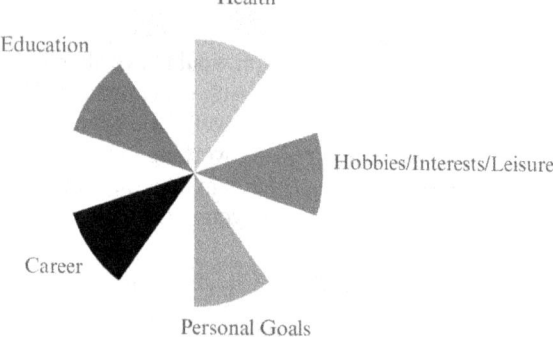

In cases where you have an injury or serious health condition, a similar domino effect can also happen. Suddenly, you can't go to work and your career has stalled. Suddenly, you can't continue with your studies. You must take time away from hobbies and loved ones just so you can recover. This all makes massive indents to your pie chart of life.

These are visual representations of why loss feels so detrimental. A piece of you and your life are gone, and maybe you weren't ready for that ending. You weren't ready to say goodbye.

RECLAIM YOUR POWER

The Pie Chart of Life (With Loss of Health)

Understanding Holistic Health – What It Is & What It Includes

Before we move onto the next exercise, I want you to understand that when we discuss health, I'm referring to holistic health as a whole. For a better understanding, take a look at the next pie chart that depicts the various facets that make up holistic health. Holistic health includes *spiritual health, emotional health, mental health, physical health, financial health, social health, intellectual health* and *environmental health.*

Components That Make Up Holistic Health

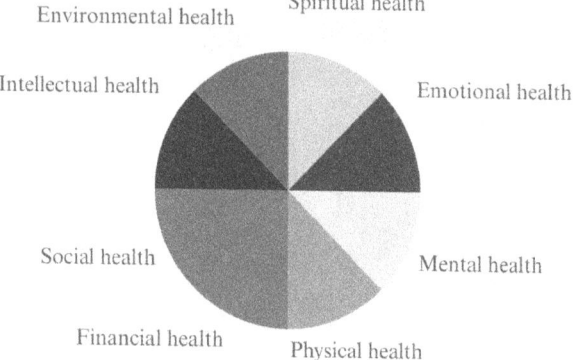

When we analyze our health, we are looking at all areas of our entire holistic health.

So what do all these components mean aside from their labels? And what does it look like to be in good health in these areas?

Let's dive into that.

Spiritual Health: A state of harmony with oneself and a connection to something greater, often involving a sense of purpose and meaning in life.

Example of what it might look like to be in good spiritual health: Regularly practicing meditation or prayer, feeling a deep sense of peace and purpose in life.

Example of what it might look like to be in poor spiritual health: Feeling a lack of purpose or meaning in life, being disconnected from one's beliefs or values, and experiencing inner turmoil.

Emotional Health: The ability to understand, manage, and express one's emotions in a healthy and constructive manner.

Example of what it might look like to be in good emotional health: Effectively coping with stress through mindfulness techniques and maintaining a positive outlook on life.

Example of what it might look like to be in poor emotional health: Frequently feeling overwhelmed by emotions, having difficulty managing stress, and experiencing frequent mood swings or persistent sadness.

Mental Health: A state of well-being in which an individual realizes their own abilities, can cope with normal stresses of life, work productively, and contribute to their community.

Example of what it might look like to be in good mental health: Seeking therapy to deal with anxiety, practicing self-care, and engaging in activities that regulate the nervous system, calming the mind.

Example of what it might look like to be in poor mental health: Struggling with persistent mental health issues such as depression or anxiety, finding it hard to concentrate, and feeling unable to cope with daily stressors.

Physical Health: The optimal functioning of the body, including regular exercise, proper nutrition, and adequate rest.

Example of what it might look like to be in good physical health: Following a balanced diet, sufficient hydration, exercising regularly, and getting optimal hours of quality sleep each night.

Example of what it might look like to be in poor physical health: Having a sedentary lifestyle, poor dietary habits, experiencing chronic illness and/or inadequate sleep leading to constant fatigue.

Financial Health: The management of financial resources to live within one's means, prepare for emergencies, and achieve financial goals.

Example of what it might look like to be in good financial health: Understanding financial literacy, having a savings account, budgeting effectively, being free from significant debt and investing long-term.

Example of what it might look like to be in poor financial health: Living paycheck to paycheck, accumulating significant debt, experiencing anxiety over financial instability, and lacking any savings for emergencies.

Social Health: The ability to form satisfying interpersonal relationships and adapt to different social situations.

Example of what it might look like to be in good social health: Maintaining strong friendships, having a supportive social network, and participating in community activities.

Example of what it might look like to be in poor social health: Feeling isolated or lonely, having strained or toxic relationships, and lacking a supportive social network.

Intellectual Health: The engagement in creative and mentally stimulating activities to expand knowledge and skills.

Example of what it might look like to be in good intellectual health: Continuously learning new things, reading books, and engaging in hobbies that challenge the mind.

Example of what it might look like to be in poor intellectual health: Not engaging in any mentally stimulating activities, feeling bored or unstimulated, and showing little interest in learning or personal growth.

Environmental Health: The environment of an individual that either positively affects their well-being.

Example of what it might look like to be in good environmental health: Living in a clean, safe and decluttered personal environment.

Example of what it might look like to be in poor environmental health: Living in a messy, disorganized environment or living an unsafe or abusive home.

Often, when people think about their health, they only include their physical health. Some people take into consideration their mental and emotional health too. But health in general can be applied to so many areas of life, that it's important to analyze all areas that affect our well-being. I hope this section provided some enlightenment and awareness on the areas of your life that could be needing a boost for improvement.

Assemble The Building Blocks for a Better Life

A crucial part of overcoming grief and loss is to begin setting down the foundation to a better life. Looking at your pie chart, begin to make decisions to fill up each area of your life again. What can you do to improve your health? What can you do to nurture your relationships? What can you do to redirect your focus towards your personal goals? What can you do to incorporate more leisure time and hobbies into your lifestyle?

The Pie Chart of Life

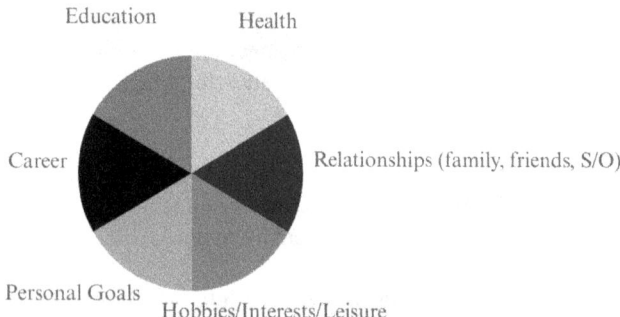

RECLAIM YOUR POWER

✧ *Build a Better Life* ✧

In this exercise, you will be ranking each area of your current holistic health then brainstorming up ideas on what you can do to build on the areas that need improvement.

Next, you'll do the exact same thing and rank each component of your current life, then come up with ways on how you can improve those areas of your life.

This activity is perfect for those who are currently going through grief and loss, but also relevant to those who aren't and simply just want to enrich their lives.

Step 1: Rank the following parts of your holistic health on a scale of 0-10.
0=Needs improvement
10= In perfect condition

Spiritual Health	___/10
Emotional Health	___/10
Mental Health	___/10
Physical Health	___/10
Financial Health	___/10
Social Health	___/10
Intellectual Health	___/10
Environmental Health	___/10

Step 2: For each health component that is not a perfect 10/10, list some ways you can improve this area of your health.

<u>*Ways to improve:*</u>

Spiritual Health

Emotional Health

Mental Health

Physical Health

Financial Health

Social Health

Intellectual Health

Environmental Health

RECLAIM YOUR POWER

Step 3: Rank the following parts of your current life on a scale of 0-10.
0=Lacking and needs improvement
10=Perfect and fulfilling

Holistic Health	___/10
Relationships (family, friends, S/O)	___/10
Hobbies/Interests/Leisure	___/10
Personal Goals	___/10
Career	___/10
Education	___/10

Step 4: For each component of life that is not a perfect 10/10, list some ways you can improve this area of your life.

<u>*Ways to improve:*</u>

Holistic Health	_____
Relationships	_____
Hobbies/Interests/Leisure	_____
Personal Goals	_____
Career	_____
Education	_____

Step 5: Make a commitment to yourself to work on improving your entire holistic health and each component of your life's pie chart.

The more you work on enriching your life, the more you will heal from grief and loss. By working on all the things that are important to you, you'll build a life you'll fall in love with. To fill up the hole in your heart that was once occupied by something or someone that is now lost, you must fill it up with the things that bring you joy.

Take this time in your journey of healing to put down the building blocks towards a better, happier and healthier life. Slowly but surely, in time you will heal.

RECLAIM YOUR POWER

Chapter 6 Key Points

- **Key Point 1:** Self-love can be a healthy support for overcoming periods of grief and loss. Learn the techniques and apply them to your daily life to support you through challenging times.
- **Key Point 2:** Self-love is even more critical to practice for those who experience fear of abandonment, codependency and/or anxious-attachment. When others have abandoned you, it's important you do not abandon yourself.
- **Key Point 3:** Offer yourself the same loving kindness and understanding you would to a good friend. Validate your own emotions and experience.
- **Key Point 4:** Be kind to yourself in the way you speak about yourself and the way you think about yourself. Your subconscious mind takes everything you think and say very literally. Change your dialogue to be supportive and empowering.
- **Key Point 5:** Take time to practice self-care during your healing journey. It doesn't matter if you think you have no time, or if others depend on you, you must fill up your own cup and tend to your needs to be able to help support others too.
- **Key Point 6:** The key to overcoming loss and grief is to fill up the piece of the pie chart that went missing when you lost something or someone meaningful.
- **Key Point 7:** Holistic health is the embodiment of spiritual health, emotional health, mental health, physical health,

financial health, social health, intellectual health and environmental health.

"Emotions are energy in motion. To release emotions, you must feel them to go through them. But too much of anything is never a good thing. Make space to feel and release your emotions, but don't stay down in that pit for too long. Know when to draw the line and continue to move forwards and upwards in life."
- Andrena Liu

Andrena Liu

CHAPTER SEVEN

SELF-LOVE IN THE ROLE OF FORGIVENESS

Andrena Liu

Forgiveness Frees the Burden

Resentment is a slow killer. It's a slow burner; a simmering pot tucked away in a back room of your life, waiting to seep out to burn the first person that touches it.

Sometimes we forget that it's there. We go about our days, forgetting we left that stovetop on.

Sometimes we remember that the stove is still on. And when we open the lid, it burns our eyes, and we quickly put the lid back on letting it continue boiling.

Resentment will slowly tear you down without you even realizing it. It will pour over and burn everything it touches.

Whether someone has wronged you in life, or you haven't been able to forgive yourself for a big mistake, forgiveness is the key to freeing yourself from the burdens of resentment.

Holding grudges increases stress and anxiety, straining our well-being. It steals our precious relationships and rids us of the beauty of human connection.

In severe instances, festering resentment can cause cardiovascular issues, a weakened immune system, sleep problems, risk of chronic conditions, social isolation, stunted personal growth, decreased self-esteem, lack of inner peace, reduced quality of life and lack of fulfilment.

In life, we will all experience being hurt and hurting others, whether we intend to or not. We will be both the giver and the receiver at some point in our lives.

RECLAIM YOUR POWER

Learning forgiveness will make it easier to overcome and move past these inevitable pains.

Forgiveness isn't approving of one's wrongdoings or letting it just slide. It doesn't mean you have to agree with the actions of another. It simply allows you to rest and be at peace in your soul. It's a mental switch of perspectives that accepts things for what they are; the good, the bad, and the ugly. It doesn't mean you allow terrible things to happen. It just means that you understand that terrible things can and will happen in life, but holding onto resentment will only ruin your own mental peace.

You can forgive others, and still fight for justice. You can forgive others, and still advocate for those who need help. You can forgive others, and still try to make things right.

You can forgive yourself, and still hold yourself accountable to be better. You can forgive yourself, so that you can move forward in your life.

There are two major reasons why you should forgive:
1. To give yourself peace.
2. To reconcile meaningful relationships.

Forgiveness is a gift to yourself.
It gives you the space to grow in life while maintaining a state of inner peace.
We may understand that forgiveness has the power to let us break free from these burdens, but why is it still so hard to do?

How to Forgive Someone Who Has Hurt You (Or Yourself)

As we've discussed in the previous section, forgiveness holds the key to reconciling meaningful relationships and it can gain us our inner peace back. You may consciously understand that you need to forgive, and maybe you really want to as well, but sometimes it's easier said than done. You want to forgive, let go and move on. But you can't get past all the hurt, anger, pain and resentment. There are a few things you can try.

H.E.A.R.T. – A Framework to Forgive Others

Once you decide you are ready to release yourself from the pain and to forgive someone for what they've done, you might want to try this framework in order. I've put together a 5-step healing process on what you can do to get to a state of understanding and forgiveness towards others.

H – **Honor** your feelings and thoughts. Validate your experience. (Tactics: Journal out what happened, your thoughts and how it made you feel OR vent to a trusted friend or mental health professional.)

E – **Empathize** with the other party. Switch to their perspective and try to understand where they were coming from. Consider the circumstances that might have influenced the other person's actions. Reflect on whether you might have responded in a similar way if you were in their situation.

A – **Appreciate** moments when you were granted forgiveness. Reflect on the times you have made mistakes and others forgave you for them. Remember how it was like to have made a mistake, and what a blessing it was to have been given grace for it.

R – **Release** and replace anger with acceptance. Accept what is. You may have to accept the loss of an idea or fantasy you once had, or the person you once knew, or the time and energy you invested, or the fact that the other person may not ever truly understand how much they hurt you.

T – **Time**, the oldest classic healer known to mankind. If all else fails, let time heal on its own.

G.R.O.W. – A Framework to Forgive Yourself

If the person needing forgiveness from yourself is you, the *G.R.O.W.* framework that I've put together may be suitable for you to try.

G – **Gain** the insights and lessons learned from your mistake.

R – **Responsibility.** Hold yourself accountable for the next time life tests you with another similar event. Don't make the same mistake next time. Lessons are repeated until they are learned.

O – **Offer** yourself compassion for what you were going through or thinking at the time. Your judgment or behavior may have been influenced by self-protection. Maybe you did the best you could in the state you were in, with the knowledge and resources you had at that time.

W – **Wisdom.** Apply the wisdom gained to future situations.

Andrena Liu

*Ho'oponopono: A Hawaiian Prayer for
Reconciliation, Forgiveness & Deep Healing*

Ho'oponopono is an ancient Hawaiian prayer and meditation for reconciliation, forgiveness and deep healing. It can help mend relationships with others and the relationship you have with yourself. It focuses on repeating 4 mantras: "I'm sorry, please forgive me, thank you, I love you."

It is a highly effective practice to help people heal their relationships and feelings of hurt and resentment.

Whether there is conflict between you and another being, or you have wronged yourself and wish to make amends, this prayer can be a miracle in reconciliation.

✧ *Ho'oponopono for Forgiveness* ✧

To practice Ho'oponopono to forgive others or yourself, ensure you are in a private quiet space, free from any possible distractions. For an auditory experience, you may also play Ho'oponopono songs from Spotify, Apple Music, YouTube or any other music streaming program.

Step 1: In a comfortable and quiet seated position, take a few deep breaths and slowly begin to close your eyes.

Step 2: In your mind or out loud, repeat each mantra, focusing on feeling into it genuinely and allow any emotions to rise.

"I'm sorry

RECLAIM YOUR POWER

Please forgive me

Thank you

I love you"

Step 3: Repeat Step 2 seven to eight times or more, taking your time to really be present with each mantra.

Step 4: End this practice with a moment of silence to integrate the message. Slowly open your eyes.

Alternatively, you may also listen to Ho'oponopono songs or write the mantras in your journal.

Write a Forgiveness Letter

To practice forgiveness, you may choose to write a forgiveness letter to the person who hurt you, or to yourself. You don't have to send this letter to them. It's just for your own way of gaining closure.

On a piece of paper or a digital document, address the letter to the one who hurt you.

You can write about what the person did, how it made you feel, what you wished they did instead, and why this was so impactful to you.

You may write that you understand why they did what they did, and that you forgive them for what happened. Express your empathy and understanding. Offer your forgiveness and your intention of moving forward. Remember to write from your heart, then close your letter off with sincerity and love.

Journaling Prompts for Forgiveness

Journaling is a tried-and-true classic practice used to sort through any conflicts in life. It can also be effective in practicing forgiveness.

Below are a list of journaling prompts that you can use in your own time to reflect on what burdens you may be carrying and why it's important to release them.

<u>For those who hurt you:</u>
1. Who do you hold resentment towards right now?
2. How have they wronged you?
3. How did it make you feel?
4. What do you think was the person's underlying intention?
5. Do you believe this person had a positive motive for what they did? Even if not, try to brainstorm a positive motive behind this person's actions.
6. What do you wish this person would say to you right now to make amends?
7. Could it be true that this person didn't know any better at the time?
8. Could it be true that this person did not intend to hurt you in this way?

RECLAIM YOUR POWER

<u>For self-forgiveness:</u>
1. What do you regret most?
2. How are your regrets impacting your life?
3. Who do you owe an apology to?
4. What was the positive motive behind the actions you regret?
5. What would happen if you never forgive yourself?

Diving deep into these journaling prompts is a very powerful psychological way to reframe bitter thoughts to thoughts of understanding and empathy. It's a very powerful tool used by counselors and therapists from a psychotherapy method called CBT (cognitive behavioral therapy).

Try to spend some time exploring these questions and see if this practice helps ease the bitter feelings replacing them with more acceptance and inner peace.

What If the Person I'm Forgiving Doesn't Change?

We can't control other people's actions and behaviors. People have free will, and sometimes they may continue to disappoint us. The point of forgiving others is not conditional on them changing. The purpose of forgiveness is so you can experience peace and healing. Forgive for your own sake, not for them.

Andrena Liu

The Value of Love in Healing Relationships

Love is a powerful value that can heal relationships. If you consider love to be one of your core values, it's important to stay true to this value. Let love guide you. Let love guide you to forgive others. Relationships don't heal when both parties turn their backs on each other. Relationships can only heal if at least one person decides to stand in unwavering love and push to resolve their issues.

In any relationship setting, issues don't resolve themselves in the presence of anger, hate and resentment. Relationships can only be saved when someone decides to let love, compassion and forgiveness mend what's broken.

You may not be able to decide what someone else does and says. But you have the power to decide for yourself right now to let things stay in the past because a special relationship is worth saving.

Remember that forgiveness doesn't mean you need to necessarily agree with what others have said and done. Forgiveness just means that you choose to be at peace and that salvaging this human connection with another being is worth more than discarding it to the ashes.

I once interviewed several people who proudly boasted lifelong decades of long-term friendships. I asked them what they said was the key to holding on to lifelong friendships, and this is what they said: Every human being makes mistakes. No one is perfect. Forgive them, accept them for who they are, and love them unconditionally. This is the key to having long-term friendships that last a lifetime.

RECLAIM YOUR POWER

Sometimes a special relationship requires you to put your own ego aside, and to step up to the plate to try to make amends. If both parties are in their own egos waiting for the other person to beg for them to come back, the relationship may not ever be salvaged. Is it really worth losing?
It only takes one person to put their own ego aside and to come forward with love, forgiveness, compassion and a willingness to make amends. Sometimes the ball is in your court and you don't even realize it.

Why Bother Asking for Forgiveness

Asking for forgiveness is a very humbling act. A lot of the times, we are so up in our egos that we can't put our pride aside, and that sabotages meaningful relationships.

The act of asking for forgiveness is full of honor because it reflects a commitment to integrity, humility and respect in relationships. It involves recognizing and owning up to your mistakes, demonstrating respect and humility, and committing to personal and relational growth.

Asking for forgiveness requires you to acknowledge that you've made a mistake or caused harm. This act of acknowledgment is honorable because it demonstrates that you are taking responsibility for your actions, rather than avoiding or deflecting blame.

It takes humility to admit that you were wrong and to seek forgiveness. This humility is a key aspect of honor, as it shows that you value the relationship and the person you've wronged more than your pride or ego.

Andrena Liu

When you ask for forgiveness, you are showing respect for the feelings and experiences of the person you've hurt. This is respectful and respectable, as it recognizes the dignity and worth of others.

Asking for forgiveness often involves a commitment to change or do better in the future. This commitment is virtuous because it shows that you are dedicated to personal growth and to improving your relationships.

By seeking forgiveness, you are actively working to restore trust and repair the relationship. This effort to make amends reflects nobility, as it demonstrates your dedication to maintaining the integrity and strength of your connections with others.

RECLAIM YOUR POWER

How to Ask for Forgiveness

Now that you understand the importance of why you should ask for forgiveness, you can follow these 4 pillars as a guideline on how to do so.

The 4 Pillars of Asking for Forgiveness

1. Empathy

The foundation of forgiveness begins with a deep understanding of the situation from all standpoints. This pillar emphasizes the importance of seeing beyond your own actions to recognize the emotional impact they have on others. Reflect on these journaling prompts to spark brainstorming on how the other person might be thinking and feeling:

- *What past experiences or beliefs might have shaped the other person's reactions?*
- *If you were in their shoes, how might you have responded to the situation?*
- *What needs or desires do you think the other person was trying to express?*
- *How might the other person have interpreted your actions or words during the conflict?*
- *What values or principles do you believe the other person was trying to uphold?*
- *What might the other person need in order to feel understood or heard?*
- *How can you show empathy towards the other person, even if you don't fully agree with their actions?*

2. Self-Accountability

Own up to your actions. Now is not the time to be pointing fingers or deflecting blame.

This pillar focuses on the importance of integrity and self-accountability. It's about standing firmly in the truth of what happened, without shifting blame. Integrity and accountability require you to be honest with yourself and the other person, acknowledging your role in the situation with full responsibility.

3. Sincerity and Humility

This is the heart of the apology. Humility is crucial when asking for forgiveness. It involves approaching the other person with a genuine sense of remorse and a sincere desire to make amends. This pillar emphasizes the emotional authenticity required in the forgiveness process.

4. Commitment to Growth

The final pillar is about looking towards the future. It involves a commitment to personal growth and making concrete changes to prevent the same mistakes from happening again. This pillar reinforces the idea that forgiveness is not just about resolving the past, but also about building a better future. This is the path forward.

Fully immerse yourself into understanding these 4 key pillars of asking for forgiveness. When you deeply understand the concepts and can integrate them into your conversation, it can open up the gates to a mended relationship. Remember that asking for forgiveness is an honorable and noble act. It may feel uncomfortable to do because it requires your humility.

RECLAIM YOUR POWER

But in the end, it will be worth the discomfort. The benefits outweigh the difficulties.

Don't Take Situations & People's Behaviors Personally

Oftentimes in many situations, people may say or do things that hurt us. Although our pain is a valid experience, the intention of the hurtful action may not have been deliberate. As human beings, we tend to assign meaning to everything, including the behaviors of others. One of the keys to forgiving others include the practice of not taking anything personally.

When you reflect on past relational conflicts and the times you've been hurt, you may recall incidents where someone took something personally, leading to greater pain and resentment. Recalling these incidents, what if you asked yourself these questions?

What did the other person do that hurt or offended me?
Why am I taking that personally?
What was the true intention of their actions, assuming they didn't mean to hurt me?
Why have I assigned such a significant meaning to their action?

Reflecting on the true intention of someone's actions with the assumption that they didn't deliberately try to offend or hurt you can open up your perspectives to not take it personally. A lot of the times, if there were no signs of obvious abuse or violence, people can take offense to other people's behaviors even when it had nothing to do with them. Take a moment to challenge yourself and see if you can reframe your own perspectives to allow for you to give someone more grace.

Chapter 7 Key Points
- **Key Point 1:** Resentment will slowly kill you. Forgiveness doesn't mean you agree with what others have said or done. Forgive so you can gain inner peace for yourself.
- **Key Point 2:** There are two major reasons why you should forgive: To give yourself peace and to reconcile meaningful relationships.
- **Key Point 3:** Use the H.E.A.R.T. framework to forgive others, and the G.R.O.W. framework to forgive yourself.
- **Key Point 4:** Ho'oponopono is a powerful ancient Hawaiian prayer for reconciliation, forgiveness and deep healing. Repeat the mantras "I'm sorry, please forgive me, thank you, I love you" a minimum of 7-8 times, while being deeply present with each meaning.
- **Key Point 5:** Write a forgiveness letter to the one you need to forgive. You don't have to send it.
- **Key Point 6:** Journaling prompts for forgiveness can be an effective tool to reframe bitter thoughts to ones of understanding and empathy.
- **Key Point 7:** Relationships don't heal when no one puts their ego aside. Let the value of love guide you to forgive and make amends. Special relationships are worth putting your ego aside to salvage and amend.
- **Key Point 8:** Asking for forgiveness is an honorable, noble and respectful act that can mend relationships.

- **Key Point 9:** Remember to apply the 4 pillars when asking for forgiveness: Empathy, Self-Accountability, Sincerity and Commitment to Growth.
- **Key Point 10:** If you're feeling upset or hurt over someone else's behavior, don't take it personally. Most of the time, people act based on the conflict going on in their own inner world and it has nothing to do with you.

"The act of asking for forgiveness is full of honor because it reflects a commitment to integrity, humility and respect in relationships."
- *Andrena Liu*

"Let love guide you. Let love guide you to forgive others. Relationships don't heal when both parties turn their backs on each other. Relationships can only heal if at least one person decides to stand in unwavering love and push to resolve their issues."
- Andrena Liu

Andrena Liu

CHAPTER EIGHT

SELF-ACCEPTANCE FOR ALL THAT YOU ALREADY ARE

Andrena Liu

Self-Acceptance for All That You Already Are

When you see and know your own value, you no longer feel the need to prove yourself to others. You now have self-validation that rises above any other external validation you could ever need. Fuelling your own internal validation with radical self-acceptance means you can choose to do what you want, and you don't have to worry about what others think. It means that you can chase after your own dreams without the fear of being judged. You don't need to win people over, because you are already your own winner.

There's also a fine delicate balance of striving to become a better person, but also offering love, compassion and acceptance for being a perfectly flawed human being. Self-acceptance is accepting and embracing yourself for all that you already are, with love and with compassion. Even though you can still hold yourself accountable to a higher standard and push yourself to learn, grow and evolve, you still accept yourself with unconditional love. Here, you don't have those negative limiting beliefs that are holding you back. Those demons have been defeated, and you know you are worthy of love just simply being you.

When it comes to viewing your own body, you own it. You accept it for all its strengths and weaknesses, for all its quirks and all its flaws. To love yourself, you can choose to become healthier, but you still accept your body for what it is. Your body is the one and only body that does everything for you. It is the body with the legs that take you from one destination to another, to be able to travel and see the world to be able to run, walk, jump, dance, twirl and play.

It is the body that will do anything for you even when you put it under pressure. It is the same body that takes you up mountains, swimming in lakes and running on the ground. Your body is a gift, it is so special. Your body is the same body that can make you feel beautiful, confident and sensual in it whether you're rocking a gorgeous outfit or feeling the vibe while letting loose some dance moves. Be thankful for your body. Be grateful. Embrace it.

✧ Self-Acceptance Journaling ✧

Right now, I want you to make a list of all the things you like about your body and physical characteristics. Keep adding to it, even the simple little things.

The things I like about my physical attributes are:

_____

_____

_____

_____

_____

_____

_____

_____

_____

RECLAIM YOUR POWER

✧ Self-Acceptance Journaling ✧

Next, I want you to make a list of all the things you're good at, whether you know you're good at it, or other people tell you that you are.

These are my strengths:

Now, add anything else additional that you like or love about yourself in general. The goal is to come up with as many as you can think of. The more, the better.

_____

_____

_____

_____

_____

_____

_____

_____

_____

RECLAIM YOUR POWER

Chapter 8 Key Points

- **Key Point 1:** Recognizing your own value eliminates the need to seek approval from others. Self-validation becomes more powerful than any external validation.
- **Key Point 2:** With self-acceptance, you can pursue your dreams without the fear of being judged by others. You become your own source of confidence.
- **Key Point 3:** Self-acceptance involves loving and embracing yourself as you are, while still striving for personal growth. You can push yourself to evolve while holding yourself with compassion.
- **Key Point 4:** Accepting yourself with unconditional love means overcoming limiting beliefs and recognizing your inherent worthiness of love simply for being who you are.
- **Key Point 5:** Embrace your body for its strengths, quirks, and flaws. While you can strive for better health, it's important to love and appreciate your body for all it does for you.
- **Key Point 6:** Your body is a gift that allows you to experience life, from physical activities to feeling confident and beautiful. Embracing and being grateful for your body is an essential aspect of self-acceptance.

"Fuelling your own internal validation with radical self-acceptance means you can choose to do what you want, and you don't have to worry about what others think. It means that you can chase after your own dreams without the fear of being judged. You don't need to win people over, because you are already your own winner."
- Andrena Liu

CHAPTER NINE

A HOLISTIC APPROACH TO SELF-LOVE

Holistic Self-Love: The Components That Make Up Self-Love as a Whole

Self-love can be defined in a multitude of ways. To truly embody it, it's important to understand all aspects of it in a holistic manner. Self-love as a whole is a combination of many parts, as visually depicted in the pie chart below. It includes *purposeful living, self-compassion, emotional and mental well-being, social well-being, spiritual well-being and physical well-being.*

Components of Self-Love in a Holistic Approach

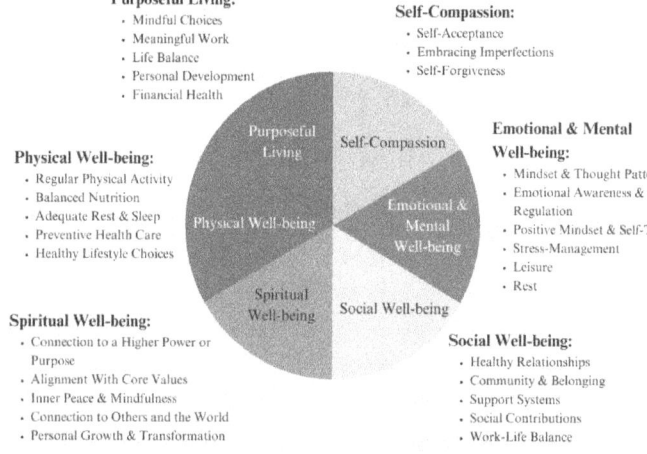

Purposeful Living:
- Mindful Choices
- Meaningful Work
- Life Balance
- Personal Development
- Financial Health

Self-Compassion:
- Self-Acceptance
- Embracing Imperfections
- Self-Forgiveness

Emotional & Mental Well-being:
- Mindset & Thought Patterns
- Emotional Awareness & Regulation
- Positive Mindset & Self-Talk
- Stress-Management
- Leisure
- Rest

Physical Well-being:
- Regular Physical Activity
- Balanced Nutrition
- Adequate Rest & Sleep
- Preventive Health Care
- Healthy Lifestyle Choices

Spiritual Well-being:
- Connection to a Higher Power or Purpose
- Alignment With Core Values
- Inner Peace & Mindfulness
- Connection to Others and the World
- Personal Growth & Transformation

Social Well-being:
- Healthy Relationships
- Community & Belonging
- Support Systems
- Social Contributions
- Work-Life Balance

1. Purposeful Living

Creating a life filled with purpose is an important aspect of self-love because it empowers you to align your actions with your values and goals. This alignment leads to a meaningful and fulfilling existence that honors your true self.

Mindful choices are about being intentional with your decisions, ensuring that each action reflects your true self and contributes to your overall well-being. Whether it's how you spend your time, the relationships you cultivate, or the habits you form, mindful choices help you live authentically and with purpose.

Meaningful work involves engaging in activities or careers that resonate with your passions and values. This type of work not only provides a sense of accomplishment but also contributes to your sense of purpose and fulfillment.

Life balance involves ensuring that you allocate time and energy to all areas of life, including work, relationships, self-care and leisure. Achieving balance allows you to live a well-rounded and harmonious life.

Personal development is the ongoing pursuit of growth and self-improvement, whether through learning new skills, exploring new experiences, or setting and achieving goals. It keeps you moving forward, constantly evolving, and becoming the best version of yourself.

Financial health is about managing your finances in a way that supports your goals and values, reducing stress, and ensuring stability. Sound financial management empowers you to make choices that align with your purpose without being hindered by financial constraints. Improving your financial literacy and pursuing financial stability are all important in maintaining good financial health.

2. Self-Compassion

Self-compassion is a fundamental component of holistic self-love. It is centered on the practice of treating yourself with the same kindness, understanding and care that you would offer to a loved one. Self-compassion is about being your own ally rather than your own worst critic.

Self-acceptance and **embracing imperfections** involve acknowledging your own suffering, mistakes, and imperfections without harsh judgment or criticism. It's loving and accepting who you already are, and where you already are. Body positivity, celebrating your achievements and recognizing your strengths are all ways to practice self-acceptance.

Self-forgiveness plays a crucial role in being compassionate towards yourself. It involves letting go of grudges and guilt that you hold against yourself for past mistakes or perceived shortcomings. By forgiving yourself, you free up emotional energy that can be used for growth and positive change.

3. Emotional & Mental Well-being

Emotional and mental well-being encompasses the health and balance of your thoughts, feelings, and psychological state. It involves understanding and managing your emotions, maintaining a positive mindset, and cultivating resilience to cope with life's challenges. Emotional and mental well-being is about creating an inner environment that supports peace, happiness, and fulfillment.

Mindset and thought patterns can contribute to the health of our emotional and mental well-being. Cultivating a healthy mindset and positive thought patterns is essential for shaping healthy and empowering perceptions and responses to life challenges.

Emotional awareness and regulation allow you to understand and manage your emotions effectively, fostering emotional resilience.

Positive mindset and self-talk reinforce a constructive mindset, helping to build self-esteem and reduce negative thinking.

Effective stress-management techniques are crucial for maintaining mental clarity and emotional well-being when facing the stress and pressures of life.

Leisure activities provide the necessary relaxation and rejuvenation required for overall well-being.

Rest, including adequate sleep, is vital to support mental and emotional healthy by allowing the body and mind to recover and recharge.

4. Social Well-being

Social well-being involves thriving in healthy relationships, feeling a sense of community and belonging, having strong support systems, making meaningful social contributions, and maintaining a balanced work-life dynamic.

Healthy relationships provide emotional support, trust, and mutual respect, which are foundational for social well-being.

Community and belonging can foster a sense of acceptance, inclusion, connection and identity, which contributes to overall life satisfaction.

Support systems offer essential emotional and practical help for navigating through life challenges more effectively.

Social contributions can give purpose to life and strengthen your connection to community, enhancing your social well-being.

Work-life balance allows you to devote time to both professional obligations and personal relationships, ensuring a well-rounded and fulfilling life.

5. Spiritual Well-being

As an aspect of holistic self-love, spiritual well-being involves building a connection to a higher power or purpose, aligning with core values, cultivating inner peace and mindfulness, building meaningful connections with others and the world, and pursuing personal growth and transformation.

Connection to a higher power or purpose provides guidance and meaning in life.

Alignment with core values ensures that your actions and decisions reflect your true self, fostering a sense of integrity and fulfillment.

Inner peace and mindfulness help you stay grounded and centered, allowing you to navigate life's challenges with calm and clarity.

Connection to others and the world enhances your sense of belonging and interconnectedness, enriching your spiritual life.

Personal growth and transformation encourages continuous evolution, helping you to reach your fullest potential and deepen your spiritual well-being.

6. Physical Well-being

In a holistic approach to self-love, physical well-being involves maintaining regular physical activity, balanced nutrition, adequate rest and sleep, preventive health care, and making healthy lifestyle choices to support overall vitality and longevity.

Regular physical activity strengthens the body, decreases chances of diseases, boosts energy levels and supports overall health and fitness.

Balanced nutrition provides the essential nutrients your body needs to function optimally and maintain good health.

Adequate rest and sleep allow your body to recover, rejuvenate, and support mental and physical well-being.

Preventative health care includes regular check-ups and screenings that help detect and prevent potential health issues before they become serious.

Healthy lifestyle choices such as avoiding harmful habits, managing stress and adopting healthier habits all contribute to long-term physical health and overall well-being.

Improving All Aspects of Self-Love

We've just discussed the 6 components that make up self-love as a holistic whole. These include: *purposeful living, self-compassion, emotional and mental well-being, social well-being, spiritual well-being and physical well-being.* To truly fully and thoroughly embody self-love, it's important to not forget any areas that contribute to self-love. The greatest life project you can ever work on is yourself. And the benefits will pay long-term dividends for life.

Remember that although self-love can be detailed and complex, that you don't have to aim for perfection. It's not necessary or realistic to aim to become a perfect being. There will always be room for improvement. So give yourself grace, and don't forget to celebrate how far you've evolved throughout your journey. If you are already 1% better than the year before, celebrate that achievement. As much as we can focus on improving our futures, don't forget to celebrate how far you've come compared to the past, and don't forget to be present and cherish each current moment.

RECLAIM YOUR POWER

✧ Self-Love Commitments ✧

Now that you have a better understanding of all that encompasses self-love, what are some steps you can take to improve your life?

I want you to think about all the ways you can show some self-love to your body better…

(Example: I will go out for a walk every day.)

_____

_____

_____

_____

_____

_____

_____

I want you to think about all the ways you can show some self-love to your mind better...

(Example: I will try to catch my cognitive distortions and replace them with more empowering statements.)

RECLAIM YOUR POWER

✧ Self-Love Commitments ✧

I want you to think about all the ways you can show some self-love to your heart better…

(Example: I will be kinder and more compassionate to myself even when I feel like I disappointed or failed myself.)

_____

_____

_____

_____

_____

_____

_____

_____

I want you to think about the ways you can show some self-love to your spirit better...

(Example: I will let go of what's holding me down by forgiving others and forgiving myself.)

_____

_____

_____

_____

_____

_____

_____

_____

_____

RECLAIM YOUR POWER

By now, I hope you are filled with motivation and reason on why it is so important and crucial for you to practice self-love and self-care. If you really integrate this new mindset and make some loving choices for yourself in your life, you can truly transform your life around.

You will be free from the grips of having to please and impress everybody.

You will be fueled with self-acceptance for who you are.

You will radiate confidence because you love and accept yourself.

And you will know that all of this will be good for everyone around you, because you will be the best version of yourself to ever exist.

Other people will experience you in a better way, and you will be proud of yourself for being a better you.

Chapter 9 Key Points

- **Key Point 1:** Self-love is made up of 6 major segments: purposeful living, self-compassion, emotional and mental well-being, social well-being, spiritual well-being and physical well-being.
- **Key Point 2:** Purposeful living is a vital aspect of self-love that empowers you to align your actions with your values and goals, resulting in a meaningful and fulfilling life that reflects your true self.
- **Key Point 3:** Self-compassion is an essential element of holistic self-love, focusing on treating yourself with the same kindness, understanding, and care that you would offer to a loved one. With self-compassion, you are your own supporter instead of a critic.
- **Key Point 4:** Emotional and mental well-being involves achieving balance and health in your thoughts, feelings, and psychological state. By understanding and managing emotions, fostering a positive mindset, and building resilience, you can create an inner environment of peace and fulfillment.
- **Key Point 5:** Social well-being is about thriving in healthy relationships, experiencing a sense of community and belonging, establishing strong support systems, contributing meaningfully to society, and maintaining a harmonious work-life balance.
- **Key Point 6:** Spiritual well-being, as part of holistic self-love, is about connecting to a higher power or purpose, living in alignment with your core values, cultivating inner peace and mindfulness, fostering meaningful connections with others and the world, and

embracing continuous personal growth and transformation.
- **Key Point 7:** Physical well-being, in a holistic approach to self-love, involves engaging in regular physical activity, following balanced nutrition, ensuring adequate rest and sleep, practicing preventive health care, and making healthy lifestyle choices.

"If everyone in the world practiced more empathy, compassion and forgiveness, the world would be a much better place."
  - Andrena Liu

CHAPTER TEN

**BONUS:
FREE SELF-LOVE
BOOSTING TOOLS**

My bonus gift to you...

As a celebratory bonus for this new revision of my paperback, and my gratitude to you for picking up this book and starting your self-love journey, I wanted to include some free gifts. In this chapter, you'll find 7 of my favourite self-love boosting tools to help fuel you on your self-love journey. I hope you enjoy using all of them and truly have so fun doing them! This journey is meant to be beautiful and liberating. May this help ignite your exhilarating fire of transformation!

Tool 1: Improve your self-talk.

Notice every time you blame, shame or guilt yourself. Just notice it, then replace it with something more compassionate. Don't just do this once. Do it every time you notice yourself being harsh with yourself.

Tool 2: Create a self-love board (like a vision board, but different!)

Find positive messages from other people, print them out, cut them out and stick them onto a physical board.

Hang up your board somewhere where you can see it every day to remind yourself of how worthy, loved and valued you are.

Tool 3: Compile a *Goddess Album*

RECLAIM YOUR POWER

Gather all your favourite photos of you, the ones that make you feel empowered and beautiful, all into one album. As a bonus, reach out to photographers to book a photoshoot and let them know you are practicing self-love, and would like your photoshoot to capture the essence of your beauty. Once you get the photos, compile them into your goddess album.

Tool 4: Listen to My High-Vibe Goddess Playlist

Tap into the emotions of self-love by grooving to my high-vibrational playlist curated to ignite your inner goddess. Feel free to dance inhibited and really channel out your inner goddess energy!

Here's the link to my playlist, just type this into any web browser: **spoti.fi/3UUDtrE**

Tool 5: Give yourself a pep talk in the mirror.

Go stand in front of the mirror. Notice all the things you love about yourself, and give yourself a pep talk as if you are your own best friend hyping yourself up. This is great practice for those with low self-esteem, low confidence and insecurities. You can't say it in your head. It's much more effective when you speak the words out loud! So if you're shy, maybe try it when no one is home.

Tool 6: Book an activity (or solo trip) to do alone.

Take yourself out on a date. Book a solo activity, or a solo trip! And genuinely enjoy your time alone. Use that time to reflect on your life, on yourself, on your own journey, on the life lessons you've learned lately, on what you appreciate and are grateful for, and on what you want to accomplish in the next few years and months. Take some time to journal and reflect. Or simply just enjoy your activity in your own presence!

Tool 7: 7-Day Limiting Belief Reprogramming

1. On a piece of paper (or the next page), list all the limiting beliefs or negative beliefs you have about yourself. Leave 4-5 empty lines between each belief. (Important: Write them in PENCIL, NOT PEN).
2. Rewrite 4 empowering lines for each negative belief. (write in pen, not pencil)

(The negative beliefs are the "lies". The re-written lines are the TRUTHS you want to adopt.)

Rule: Don't use "don't" or "not".

3. Read the lies and truths every day for 7 days straight.
4. Erase the lies after 7 days.

7-Day Limiting Belief Reprogramming

Negative/limiting belief #1 (Write in pencil; Erase after 7 days):

_____
_____

New empowering thought (Write in pen):

_____
_____

New empowering thought (Write in pen):

_____
_____

New empowering thought (Write in pen):

_____
_____

New empowering thought (Write in pen):

_____
_____

Negative/limiting belief #2 (Write in pencil; Erase after 7 days):

_____
_____

New empowering thought (Write in pen):

_____
_____

New empowering thought (Write in pen):

_____
_____

New empowering thought (Write in pen):

_____
_____

New empowering thought (Write in pen):

_____
_____

Negative/limiting belief #3 (Write in pencil; Erase after 7 days):

_____
_____

New empowering thought (Write in pen):

_____
_____

New empowering thought (Write in pen):

_____
_____

New empowering thought (Write in pen):

_____
_____

New empowering thought (Write in pen):

_____
_____

Andrena Liu

CONCLUSION

THE END OF A BOOK; THE BEGINNING OF AN EVOLUTION

Andrena Liu

Closing Off With My Deepest Gratitude

As we come to a close in this journey of a book, may it not be the end of the path but an inspiration for continuous growth. Reflecting on the profound and transformative power of self-love, may we continue to integrate these lessons to our daily lives.

From understanding what self-love truly means, to exploring its deep significance in every aspect of life, this book aims to equip you with the knowledge, tools, and insights required to embrace this essential practice.

We began by defining self-love and dispelling the myths that often surround it. It is not a selfish act, but rather a selfless one that enables you to show up as your best self, not only for yourself but for others as well. By filling your own cup, you create enough overflow to positively affect the lives of those around you.

The practical techniques shared throughout these chapters are designed to be accessible and adaptable to anyone, no matter where you are in your self-love journey. These daily practices can bring about life-changing results, as they help you cultivate a deeper connection with yourself and foster an environment where healing and growth can occur.

We delved into the importance of healing past wounds and setting personal boundaries, recognizing that self-love is an ongoing process of self-discovery and self-care. By understanding and addressing your triggers, you can release the limiting beliefs that have held you back and create a life that is truly aligned with your highest self.

Through the exploration of grief, forgiveness, and the delicate balance between self-improvement and self-acceptance, we've seen how self-love is both a journey and a destination. It's about striving to become the best version of yourself while also embracing and accepting who you are at this moment.

Finally, the holistic approach to self-love presented in this book is an invitation to integrate these practices into every aspect of your life. The tools and activities provided are here to help you design a self-love routine that is uniquely yours, tailored to meet your personal needs and aspirations.

As you move forward, remember that self-love is not a one-time achievement, but a continuous, evolving process. It's about making a daily commitment to prioritize your well-being, to honor your emotions, and to celebrate your journey with kindness and compassion. May the insights and practices shared in these pages guide you toward a life filled with greater self-love, inner peace, and lasting fulfillment.

Lastly, I want to thank you, my dear reader, for the time, energy, commitment and open-mindedness you've held throughout this entire journey. I hope you are proud of yourself for opening up your mind to these new ideas and for putting in the time, energy and work. I am truly proud of you for taking accountability and following with me through to the end of this book. I hope the insights,

Andrena Liu

wisdoms, techniques and inspirational words have reached you at the right time in your life. I do believe everything happens for a reason, and this booked landed on your path by fate. Thank you for following along in this incredibly profound and personal journey. I wish you the best of luck in the rest of your growth and healing journey.

Sincerely,

Andrena Liu

BIBLIOGRAPHY

Ainsworth, M. D. S., Blehar, M. C., Waters, E., & Wall, S. (1978). Patterns of Attachment: A Psychological Study of the Strange Situation. Hillsdale, NJ: Lawrence Erlbaum Associates.

Anderson, S. (2000). The Journey from Abandonment to Healing: Surviving Through and Recovering from the Five Stages that Accompany the Loss of Love. New York: Berkley Books.

Aurelius, M. (2006). Meditations (M. Staniforth, Trans.). London: Penguin Classics. (Original work published ca. 180)

Bandler, R., & Grinder, J. (1975). The Structure of Magic: A Book About Language and Therapy. Palo Alto, CA: Science and Behavior Books.

Bandler, R., & Grinder, J. (1976). The Structure of Magic II: A Book About Communication and Change. Palo Alto, CA: Science and Behavior Books.

Beattie, M. (1986). Codependent No More: How to Stop Controlling Others and Start Caring for Yourself. Center City, MN: Hazelden.

Beck, A. T. (1976). Cognitive Therapy and the Emotional Disorders. New York: International Universities Press.

Beck, A. T., & Greenberg, R. L. (1984). Cognitive Therapy of Depression. New York: Guilford Press.

Bowlby, J. (1969). Attachment and Loss: Vol. 1. Attachment. New York: Basic Books.

Bowen, M. (1978). Family Therapy in Clinical Practice. New York: Jason Aronson.

Bradshaw, J. (1990). Homecoming: Reclaiming and Championing Your Inner Child. New York: Bantam Books.

Burns, D. D. (1980). Feeling Good: The New Mood Therapy. New York: HarperCollins.

Cloud, H., & Townsend, J. (1992). Boundaries: When to Say Yes, How to Say No to Take Control of Your Life. Grand Rapids, MI: Zondervan.

Ellis, A. (1962). Reason and Emotion in Psychotherapy. New York: Lyle Stuart.

Hayes, S. C., Strosahl, K. D., & Wilson, K. G. (1999). Acceptance and Commitment Therapy: An Experiential Approach to Behavior Change. New York: Guilford Press.

Jeffers, S. (1987). Feel the Fear and Do It Anyway. New York: Ballantine Books.

Jonas, W. B., & Levin, J. S. (Eds.). (1999). Essentials of Complementary and Alternative Medicine. Philadelphia: Lippincott Williams & Wilkins.

Mellody, P., Wells, A., & Miller, J. K. (1989). Facing Codependence: What It Is, Where It Comes from, How It Sabotages Our Lives. New York: Harper & Row.

Miller, A. (1979). The Drama of the Gifted Child. New York: Basic Books.

Naperstek, B. (2004). Invisible Heroes: Survivors of Trauma and How They Heal. New York: Bantam Dell.

Nicholls, G. (n.d.). CBT (Cognitive Behavioural Therapy) Coach Practitioner Certification. The Priority Academy.

OpenAI. (2024). ChatGPT (August 13, 2024 version) [Large language model]. Retrieved from https://www.openai.com/chatgpt

OpenAI. (2024). List of subconscious limiting beliefs. ChatGPT. https://www.openai.com/chat

Rivera, J., Rivera, N., & Key, D. (n.d.). NLP Certification and NLP Practitioner Life Coach Training. Transformation Academy.

Rivera, J., & Rivera, N. (n.d.). Professional Life Coach Certification. Transformation Academy.

Ruiz, D. M. (1997). The Four Agreements: A Practical Guide to Personal Freedom. San Rafael, CA: Amber-Allen Publishing.

Singer, M. A. (2007). The Untethered Soul: The Journey Beyond Yourself. Oakland, CA: New Harbinger Publications.

van der Kolk, B. A. (2014). The Body Keeps the Score: Brain, Mind, and Body in the Healing of Trauma. New York: Viking.

Vitale, J., & Hew Len, I. (2007). Zero Limits: The Secret Hawaiian System for Wealth, Health, Peace, and More. Hoboken, NJ: Wiley.

Weil, A. (1995). Spontaneous Healing: How to Discover and Enhance Your Body's Natural Ability to Maintain and Heal Itself. New York: Knopf.

TO CONTACT THE AUTHOR

If you would like to contact the author, you may write to her at contact@andrenaliu.com. The author would be happy to hear how this book has affected you.

CONNECT ON SOCIAL MEDIA

Stay updated with Andrena by following her on Instagram, TikTok and Youtube at @andrenaliu.

For more information, please visit
www.andrenaliu.com

www.ingramcontent.com/pod-product-compliance
Lightning Source LLC
Chambersburg PA
CBHW050527170426
43201CB00013B/2110